A Cook's Guide to
CHINESE VEGETABLES

A Cook's Guide to
CHINESE VEGETABLES

Martha Dahlen

Illustrated by Karen Phillipps

Copyright © 1992 renewed by Martha Dahlen

This edition published in 1992 by The Guidebook Company Ltd, Hong Kong

Distribution in the United Kingdom and Ireland, Europe and certain Commonwealth countries by Hodder & Stoughton, Mill Road, Dunton Green, Sevenoaks, Kent TW13 2YA
Distribution in Hong Kong and China by Pacific Century Publishers Limited, tel. 811 5505, fax. 565 8624

British Library Cataloguing-in-Publication Data
A catalogue record for this book is available from the British Library

Designed by Teresa Ho
Production House: Twin Age Limited, Hong Kong

Printed in China

Table of Contents

Foreword

...PAST

The volume you hold is this book's fourth incarnation. It was originally written and published in Hong Kong as two volumes entitled *A Guide to Chinese Market Vegetables* and *A Further Guide to Chinese Market Vegetables*. A consolidated version, *A Popular Guide to Chinese Vegetables*, was produced in 1982 and sold internationally until it went out of print in 1990.

...PRESENT

This new, and entirely rewritten, edition covers not only shopping and cooking but also assesses the nutritional value of each vegetable—according to Chinese concepts. Throughout, the emphasis is on practical information. For the experimental cook and vegetable gourmet, Asian markets are treasure troves. The seasonal variety of greens, melons, roots and fruits amazes the eye, teases the palate—and could leave the mind bewildered. 'It must be edible, but what is it? How do I choose a good one? How should it be prepared?' The following pages attempt to answer these questions clearly and concisely.

Each vegetable description includes cooking advice for preparing the vegetables in both Western and Chinese styles; many include recipes. For the most part, both advice and recipes were gleaned while eating with Hong Kong families, watching amahs and mothers cook, and listening to the advice of friends and vegetable vendors. Consequently, the 'recipes' tend to be basic, general guidelines rather than elaborate formulae; they require only a couple of versatile pots and simple seasoning. Royal chefs (and Chinese restaurants) may prepare elaborate dishes from exotic ingredients, but the essence of quality is still the small-scale, experienced technique and fresh ingredients with which they work.

Finally, as mentioned above, the following pages include brief comments on the vegetables in terms of Asian concepts of nutrition. The essential nature of the foodstuff and its effect on the body are not only fundamental to Chinese cooking, but also integral to every housewife's common sense about cooking. Hence, they influence what ingredients are cooked together, in what season they are served, and to whom they are served.

Be that as it may, the fact remains that good cooking depends on understanding—whether intellectually or intuitively—the nature of your ingredients and how to combine them to produce good flavor and nutrition. The Chinese approach can open new doors, and these nutritional comments are primarily intended to inspire and guide your own creative efforts in the kitchen.

...FUTURE

Armed with the illustrations and information here, anyone should be able to identify, select, prepare and cook these vegetables with confidence. Familiarity may breed contempt, but in this case it should become a bridge between ignorance and bliss for those who enjoy good food.

Acknowledgements

Of the many people who have contributed to this book—some knowingly, others not, some through their knowledge, others through their skill—one deserves public acknowledgement for her indefatigable willingness to help. Betty Ng, thanks.

Names

Be warned that the romanized names on the following pages will probably not match names on bottles and packages, or even in other books. The romanized spellings given here represent Cantonese pronunciation rendered in the most simple yet accurate form possible; names on bottles may be written according to any of a number of different formal linguistic systems, or may be of another Chinese dialect, or may be other names altogether. These differences, while frustrating, cannot be helped because any attempt to render a two-dimensional (i.e. tonal) language like Chinese with a one-dimensional alphabet like the roman will be artificial and approximate.

The solution to identification, then, is to rely less on the written word. If you can recognize what you want, the written word is irrelevant. Where this is not possible and/or words are necessary, match pronunciations not spellings. For instance, *baak choi* sounds like 'bok choy'; *dau see* vaguely approximates 'dou shih'. Better yet, and for absolute accuracy, match the Chinese characters.

Chinese Cooking Utensils

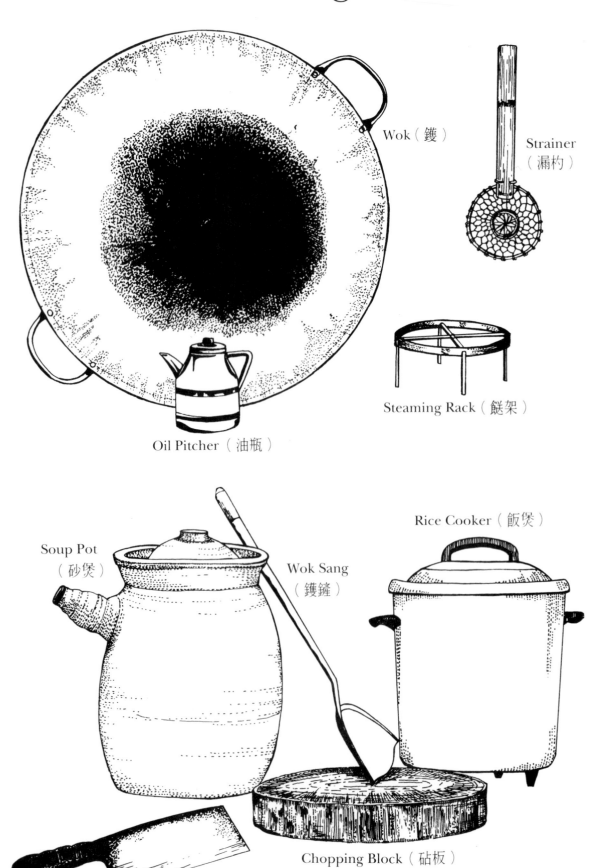

Wok（鑊）

Strainer（漏杓）

Oil Pitcher（油瓶）

Steaming Rack（餸架）

Soup Pot（砂煲）

Wok Sang（鑊鏟）

Rice Cooker（飯煲）

Chopping Block（砧板）

Chopper（菜刀）

Basic Chinese Cooking Methods

COOKING RICE

Undoubtedly the greatest, and possibly the only revolutionary, gift modern science has given to Chinese home cuisine is the electric rice cooker. Cookers range in size from two-man, six-bowl capacity to those used in restaurants capable of cooking rice for thirty. But rice cookers can do more than just cook rice; they can also boil soup, simmer congee, and steam dishes in ways that render other pots unnecessary and that make cooking three-course meals possible in offices, shops and dorm rooms.

Rice cookers today come in an assortment of shapes and sizes with a variety of features. The most simple, common (and easy to clean) kind consists of a removable insert that holds rice and water, and the pot body that contains the heating element, thermostat and control switches outside. To use the cooker, place the desired quantity of raw rice in the insert, rinse it three times to remove excess starch, and then add cooking water. Measure water either (1) by volume, in which case use equal quantities rice and water for white rice, or twice as much water as rice for brown rice; or (2) by hand, in which case, when the fingertips rest lightly on the submerged surface of the raw rice, the water level should reach halfway between the first and second knuckle of the middle finger.

Having added rice and water, set the insert in the cooker body, replace the lid, and depress the 'cook' button. The light inside the button will glow, indicating the heating element is on. When the rice is cooked—or, more precisely, when the temperature of the pan rises above the boiling point of water because all water has been absorbed by the rice or steamed away—cooking stops. At this point, depending on the cooker model, the heating element may go off altogether or it may switch to 'warm' mode.

Brown rice requires more attention because it naturally takes longer to cook; in the above scenario, the water will be steamed away before the grains have a chance to absorb it. To avoid this, stop the cooking manually after the rice has come to a boil; let rest 10–15 minutes; then resume to complete the cooking.

To cook rice in a saucepan, rinse rice and measure water as described above, bring to the boil, then reduce heat to the absolute minimum. With a cast-iron pot, you can even turn off the heat altogether because the pan will retain enough heat to cook the rice. Alternatively, use a double boiler.

In all cases, if you want tender, separate grains, do NOT stir the rice after it has begun to cook. If the rice cooks dry before it is done, moisten it by adding small amounts of hot water, preferably by drizzling it around the edge of the pan. The idea is to get the water down to the bottom, from where it will rise as steam to swell the grains gently. It is better to add a little water several times than a larger quantity all at once—again, because the idea is to generate steam to cook the upper layers, not to stew the bottom layers.

SEASONING RAW MEAT

Chop chicken into bite-size pieces, preferably strips; cut beef or pork across the grain into thin strips. Mix the meat with pinches of salt, sugar, cornstarch; a drizzle of light soy sauce, and—last but not least—enough oil to render the bits separate and shiny.

This seasoning procedure is fairly universal and is done anytime from ten minutes to an hour before cooking. In the recipes that follow, 'meat, seasoned' means to prepare it as described above.

SEASONING FRESH FISH, SHRIMP OR PRAWNS, AND ORGAN MEATS

Fresh whole fish should be scaled, cleaned, rinsed with water, and rubbed lightly with (coarse) salt. Shrimp, cleaned or whole, should be rinsed to clean and tossed with (coarse) salt to remove slime and to firm the flesh. Juice of freshly grated ginger, shreds of fresh ginger soaked in wine, and white pepper are all reputed to kill off-flavors of less-than-fresh fish and liver. Thus, use them in marinades for shredded liver and other organ meats, chopped fish and shrimp before cooking. Soy sauce is generally not used with white flesh so as not to spoil the color.

STIR-FRYING

This is a two-step technique: first, the food is lightly tossed in hot oil to seal flavors in; second, it is quickly cooked by steam. Intense heat and speed are the keys to success. Here is how to do it:

Heat the wok*. Add oil according to the quantity and type of food you will cook; experience and taste will teach you proportions. When the oil is quite hot and beginning to smoke, tip the wok to coat all surfaces that food will hit with hot oil.

At this point, add any crushed garlic or ginger called for; toss until fragrant and then discard. Add the washed, drained, chopped vegetables all at once. A loud, continuous hiss should reverberate through the kitchen. The quality, volume, and duration of this sound is often directly proportional to the quality of the finished dish. As soon as you have added pieces of food to the wok, begin tossing them with the *wok-sang* in order to coat them quickly and evenly with oil. When they begin to cook, becoming fragrant, wilted, and bright in color, sprinkle with salt. Leafy veg will be done after another minute or two of tossing. For more solid vegetables, add a little water to create steam, and clamp the lid on. When you judge the vegetables are done, remove the lid, toss them, and correct the seasoning. The vegetables taste and look better if you lift the lid only once, when they are done; there should be virtually no liquid remaining.

In a mixture, add slow-cooking ingredients first, or stir-fry them separately. With mixed meat and vegetables, the Cantonese generally stir-fry the meat first, remove; then the veg; returning the meat to toss with the veg just before dishing up.

N.B. Proper stir-frying depends on having a hot pan. This means (1) a heat source strong enough to maintain intense heat throughout the cooking process; and (2) a pan that holds an even heat. The concave shape of the wok distributes the heat over a large surface area, accommodates large and small volumes of food, withstands sudden changes of temperature, and encourages quick evaporation.

However, despite its attributes, a wok may not be the best utensil for stir-frying in your home. The best woks are made of iron or steel. Inferior woks are made of aluminum, often coated with teflon. The metal heats unevenly and the teflon coating interferes with evaporation; both challenge even accomplished chefs—much less novices—to cook well. Furthermore, on electric burners the metal collar used to support the wok invariably raises it so far from the heat that it can never reach proper stir-frying temperature. Under these conditions, a cast-iron skillet with tall sides or a sturdy saucepan may be your best cooking utensil.

In any case, note that stir-frying is not the only method of cooking Chinese food, and if it is invariably disappointing in your kitchen, try more braised, steamed, or deep-fried dishes.

DEEP-FRYING

The critical factor here is temperature. The oil must be hot enough to cook the ingredients quickly without soaking them in oil, but not hot enough to burn the outside before the inside is cooked. The quantity of oil must be enough such that adding food does not drop its temperature below the critical oil-soaking temperature.

In practice this means: (1) Use at least four times as much by volume of oil as ingredients to be fried at one time. (2) Heat it to the appropriate temperature. Chinese cooks use a bamboo chopstick as a thermometer—when a bamboo chopstick inserted in the middle of the oil causes bubbles to rise around it, the oil is ready. (3) Foods to be fried should be cut in uniform, small or thin pieces, kept dry, and added in small quantities.

STEAMING

This technique is used particularly for fresh fish, savoury egg custards, rice flour puddings, and seasoned meat mixtures. Accomplish it as follows:

Place a steaming rack in a pot. The rack may be a purchased one as illustrated, anything comparable you can fashion from sturdy wire, or a brick; in a wok you may also use a grid or a pair of sticks wedged in about 1/3 of the way up the wok's sides. Fill the pot with 1–2 inches of water, cover, and bring to a boil. When the water reaches a rolling boil, place the dish of prepared food on the rack, re-cover the pot, and maintain the water at a gentle boil until the food is cooked. Alternatively—and more commonly among Cantonese—the rack is set in the rice cooker so that the dish cooks in the steam of the cooking rice.

Shallow round enamelled or stainless steel pans are the most convenient dishes to use for steaming food because they are unbreakable and conduct heat quickly. In Hong Kong, most Cantonese households have a nested series of such pans varying in diameter from 3 to 8 inches— and most have a rice cooker twice as big as necessary in order to have room above the rice for steaming dishes.

In restaurants, steaming is done with bamboo steamers over woks of boiling water. The steamers come in sections, each section consisting of a circumference of bamboo and a grid inside to support the food. The sections fit on top of each other, with a lid to terminate the stack. Bamboo is better than metal as a steaming container because it absorbs and leaks water, rather than causing it to condense and drip onto the food.

CREATING CANTONESE GRAVY

To thicken a sauce or to make Cantonese *heen*, combine cornstarch with 2–3 parts cold water, mix to homogeneity, add to the hot food while stirring, and cook for a minute or two until it thickens. Generally 2–3 teaspoons of cornstarch will thicken 1 cup of liquid to a medium consistency.

Chinese Cooking Nutrition

Preparing a meal is neither random nor whimsical in a Chinese household. Certain patterns, principles, and what seem to be regulations govern choices of the foods to serve and how to prepare them.

The first pattern is the composition of the menu: in a typical Cantonese evening meal there will be steamed rice, dishes of meat and/or vegetables (ideally the same number of dishes as there are diners), and a soup. The soup will be invariably a broth, ideally the result of several hours of boiling, and generally derived from a combination of meat or bones, some fresh and some dried ingredients. While rice is the *sine qua non* of the meal, the soup is the *sine qua joie*—a source of real pleasure as well as of nutrition.

The principles for choosing what to prepare are grounded in Chinese concepts of nutrition. Where Westerners look at food and see vitamins, minerals, cholesterol, and calories, the Cantonese look and see the potential for hot, cold, wet, and/or dry influences on the body's intrinsic balance. Chocolate provides a good contrast in the two interpretations. According to the Western view, chocolate is rich in oil and sugar, is therefore fattening and causes pimples. According to the Chinese view, chocolate is 'heating', therefore causing hot eruptions on the skin. Cucumbers, in contrast, are 'cooling' and can be eaten to restore balance in an 'overheated' body.

Applying criteria of temperature and humidity to food seems foreign to the Westerner, but is pre-eminent common sense to the Cantonese. Chinese concepts of nutrition are the same as Chinese concepts of medicine, and both are based on Chinese philosophy. As the Chinese look out on life, they see the same fundamental principles governing the weather as well as plants, animals, and people. The dynamic polarity of 'yin' and 'yang' are often mentioned in this context, as are the 'organ-meridians' of acupuncture along which vital energy flows, creating life. The third universal organizing principle includes the two sets of opposites, hot/cold and wet/dry, and it is these that become the dietary guidelines for the average man on the street—and cook in the kitchen. Western people are quite familiar with these as characteristics of the weather or as temporary conditions of their body or food; Chinese use these labels for intrinsic properties of both food and bodies.

'Warming' foods generate heat in the body. On the good side, this means they can stimulate metabolism, keep the extremities warm, produce energy, etc. On the bad side, they can encourage inflammation (e.g. sore throat, ulcers) and exacerbate infections; redness is a typical symptom of excess heat. Examples of such foods are beef, chestnuts, carrots, ginger; in general, it seems, the more dense the food the more likely it is to be classified as warming.

In contrast, 'cooling' foods produce smooth, sliding effects. On the good side, this means cleansing and prevention or relief of toxic heat; losing excess weight. On the bad side, this could mean diarrhea, runny nose, weakness. Examples are crab, cucumbers, lettuce; in general, leafy vegetables and fruits are classified as cooling.

Less familiar are the concepts of 'damp' and 'dry'. Dampness in the body manifests as water retention, tendency toward skin problems (e.g. oozing sores, fungal infections), arthritic aches and pains. Dryness manifests as thirst, dry cough, dry skin, constipation. In other words, this simply says that different vegetables and styles of cooking will tend to affect the water balance of the body—i.e. generating 'dampness' or 'dryness'—differently.

Although these concepts seem foreign, they are already part of Western common sense and even language—e.g. 'cool as a cucumber'. For Chinese they are the traditional barometer for evaluating food, and a daily consideration as seasons change and bodies grow. Where an American automatically gauges calorie content, a Hong Kong Cantonese just as automatically gauges 'heat'—not only of the food but also of the weather and his own internal state. To retooth two old saws: 'One man's heat could be another man's poison', and 'For every food there is a season.'

IN DAILY LIFE

So what does all this mean to the average housewife as she markets and prepares daily meals? Does she have yin-yang, hot-cold, wet-dry thermometers and consult charts of foods and their effects on the flow of *ch'i* in the organ-meridians? No. The wisdom of the centuries has been distilled into (generally) two-word aphorisms that virtually every Cantonese seems to pick up as they grow up.

'Ginger?' 'Expels wind,' comes the reply. 'Soy beans?' 'Cold and dry.' 'Green radish?' 'Drains energy.' And so it goes. Similarly, there are conventions that approach the status of culinary statutes as to what is cooked with what, and how. Certain vegetables are boiled in soup, never stir-fried or braised. Others are always stir-fried, never boiled. Some go with garlic or beef, others only taste 'right' with pork. When examined in the light of Chinese medical characterisations of the vegetables, the rules make sense. Ginger ('warming' and wind-expelling) goes with soy beans ('cold' and wind-inducing). But most Chinese don't bother with sense. They just know you have to add ginger when you cook soy beans or they won't taste good and you won't feel right afterward.

IN THIS BOOK

In view of how fundamental Chinese nutritional concepts are to their cooking, the descriptions in this book include basic comments along these lines. In general, they are what the average person knows and are based on Hong Kong hearsay, with limited consultation of descriptions published by Chinese doctors. It should be noted here that not all accounts agree. This is disappointing, but not surprising for a subjective, relative system. Furthermore, it emphasizes the main point: the important characteristics of a vegetable are not an independent reality; they relate to what your body does with a vegetable after you eat it. As mentioned above, the system may seem new to a Westerner, but in fact it is not. Expanding the concepts offers a means by which each individual can himself assess and modify his diet for optimum nutrition. Furthermore, as for the Chinese, the rules offer the newcomer sensible guidelines—the wisdom of generations of cooks—in exploring the culinary possibilities of Chinese vegetables. *Bon santé.*

The Vegetables

GINGER *Geung* 薑

APPEARANCE: These irregularly jointed rhizomes usually measure 1/2–1 inch in diameter and have a paper-thin, beige or golden skin. Pieces vary in size from small bits to whole 'hands', so named because new growth spreads outward from the oldest, original piece like so many irregular 'fingers'.

QUALITY: Select rhizomes that are clear-skinned and robust, with no sign of shrivelling or fungal rot. Examine joints where rhizomes have been freshly broken: the more and larger the protruding fibres, the older the root. Young ginger is more tender and sweet, but old ginger is considered more potent, and hence preferred for most cooking purposes.

COMMENTS: Used for its aroma, flavor and physiological effects, ginger is essential to traditional Chinese cooking. It is considered a 'yang' food because it stimulates many activities in the body, e.g. gastric secretion, blood circulation, and perspiration. More to the point here, cooks should know that it can kill offensive odours (as of not-quite-fresh fish and meat), bring out pungent flavors, eliminate wind (as generated by cabbages and beans), and disperse cold (as in the 'common cold' as well as in dishes cooked with 'cooling' ingredients). For these reasons—in addition to its flavor—ginger appears in a tremendous range of dishes, from soups and stir-fry to meat marinades.

Two further notes of peripheral interest:
First, dried ground ginger is not a good substitute for fresh ginger in Chinese cooking because it is so much stronger. The extra pungency of dried ginger derives, first, from the drying process—which, in this case, intensifies an already 'hot' nature—and second, from its origins in India, where different varieties are grown.
Second, ginger has been proven clinically effective in alleviating nausea, be it due to motion sickness, food poisoning, or surgery. Any form of ginger—fresh, dry, powdered, juiced, or candied—seems effective for this purpose.

PREPARATION: First, peel it. Cantonese cooks accomplish this by scraping the surface with the blade of a small paring knife held perpendicular to the surface. Then either slice in thin shreds; chop in coarse chunks; or grate or press in a garlic press to produce juice.

COOKING: According to the Cantonese, ginger is best boiled, braised, or steamed, but not fried outright in oil because that would excessively intensify its 'heating' qualities. Other Chinese reckon that the Cantonese are too sensitive, and that certain dishes—particularly those comprised of innately 'cooling' vegetables—need the heat. Remembering the differences, experiment for yourself.

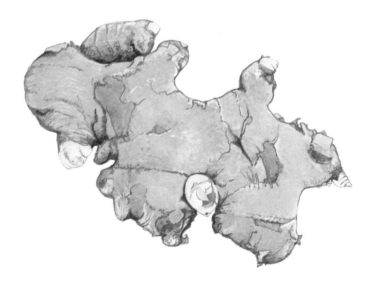

As for which dishes merit a slice or two of ginger, follow the guidelines in the 'Comments' above, i.e. consider using ginger whenever you are cooking fish, cabbage, soy beans or soy bean derivatives, and purely vegetable dishes.

Below are examples of how the Chinese use ginger, followed by a recipe for a dessert popular in Macau.

Shreds Simply float shreds in (red) vinegar to make a dip for dumplings (Shanghai) or deep-fried foods, particularly fish and seafood. (N.B. The ginger will stimulate the stomach, the vinegar will stimulate the liver—both will aid in digesting the oil.) Make the dip elaborate by adding minced spring onions, shallots, or chillies, soy sauce, sesame oil, sugar, wine, etc, according to taste.

When steaming fish, lay the shreds generously over, under and inside the fish.

Slices When stir-frying vegetables or meat, toss in fine shreds or a thin, crushed slice just as you add water, and clamp the lid on for steaming. It is particularly appropriate for bland vegetables such as bean sprouts, bean curd, lettuce, and summer melons.

To season soups and braised dishes, add crushed slice(s) as desired. Length of cooking time determines the size of the slices: for large quantities of soups to be simmered for 3–4 hours, 1-inch chunks that have been peeled and rudely smashed with the broadside of a cleaver are added; for casseroles, just a thick slice or two will do.

Juice Use ginger juice to marinate fish, squid, liver, shrimp, or chicken. Adding a little rice wine further enhances flavor.

GINGER MILK CUSTARD
Per rice-bowl of milk (approx 6 oz):
   1 egg white (or small whole egg)
   1 tbsp sugar
   1/2– 1 tsp ginger juice*
   Dash of white vinegar

*To make ginger juice, peel a small piece of fresh ginger; either crush it in a garlic press or grate it, and squeeze juice from the pulp.

To make the custard, first beat egg whites until frothy. Add milk, sugar, ginger juice, and vinegar. Beat slightly to mix. Pour milk into rice bowls, or similarly sized containers. Place in steamer, i.e. place bowls on racks over boiling water in a large pot or wok; cover. Steam over simmering water until beginning to set, 5–10 minutes. Lift lid; lower heat. After 10 minutes, custard should be virtually set. If so, extinguish heat, allow to sit covered another 15 minutes, then serve.

You may also bake the custard, with the bowls set in a tray of hot water in the oven. This takes longer but does not change the flavor.

GARLIC   *Suen tau* 蒜頭

APPEARANCE: Cloven or whole, garlic can be recognized at short range by its white papery husks and at long range by its inimitable smell when crushed.

QUALITY: Whole heads should be uniformly firm; if not, inner cloves may have dried up or been consumed by fungus. Individual cloves should be similarly full and firm, with no sign of shrivel, rot, worms, or sprouts; the larger they are, the easier to peel.

COMMENTS: Garlic is a cosmopolitan condiment, more than 5,000 years old. Asians and Europeans alike employ this brash onion for its distinct and distinctive flavor, and reap dividends of health from its pungent constituents.

According to the Chinese, garlic is a 'warming' food, a powerful tonic for the digestive and respiratory systems, and one that can kill internal 'bugs'. Hence it is a food for all seasons, and a welcome complement to a variety of vegetables. Its warmth stimulates; its pungency aerates and dries the body. All three qualities are considered desirable and appropriate in summer, when appetites flag and 'dampness' settles in the body. In colder, northern provinces raw garlic is routinely eaten to kill worms and to prevent and/or treat dysentery and pneumonia. Nevertheless, too much of a good thing is bad, and excess garlic is believed to harm the stomach and liver.

Chemically, the characteristic odour and taste of garlic derive from a reaction that occurs when a certain enzyme meets a certain substrate. Any action that breaks garlic cells immediately precipitates this fragrant union. Thus, for maximum development of flavor, garlic must be thoroughly minced or crushed.

PREPARATION: The Chinese method of crushing garlic is efficient and effective. Position unpeeled clove(s) on the chopping board, then smash it (them) with a single, swift, firm blow of the broadside of a heavy cleaver. During crushing, the husk prevents bits of garlic from scattering to all corners of the kitchen; after crushing, it readily falls away from the inner clove—which is then ready for use.

COOKING:

Western Wherever onions go, let a clove of garlic lead the way to enhance and enrich the flavor of, e.g., salad dressings, marinades, casseroles, roasts, and vegetable sautés.

Chinese The Cantonese use garlic for flavor as well as 'warmth'. It is stir-fried with leafy vegetables—particularly summer greens such as water spinach and Chinese spinach (q.v.), as well as the winter cabbages. It is crushed with fermented black beans to make the versatile black bean sauce (see below). And it is braised whole in winter casseroles.

Where only a hint of garlic is desired, the crushed clove is added to the hot oil, then removed and discarded before cooking proceeds. Or garlic shallots (q.v.) are used instead.

BLACK BEAN SAUCE
Fermented black beans (*dau see* 豆豉)*
Garlic
Soy sauce
Sugar
(Chilli)

*Note that the beans called for here are not the round, hard, turtle beans of Mexican cuisine. Chinese fermented black beans are soy beans that have been cooked, salted, and fermented in a process similar to making soy sauce; hence, they are oblong in shape, rather soft in texture, and rich in flavor.

General directions for sauce: use approximately two parts black beans to one part garlic. (Some cooks rinse the beans before proceeding.) Crush the garlic, then mince. Cantonese home-chefs then put this in a small bowl together with the black beans, and mash them together with the end of the cleaver handle; restaurant cooks don't bother, leaving the beans whole. In any case, approximately 1 tablespoon of mash will season 2 cups of food.

To cook, add the mash (or loose beans and garlic) to the hot oil before the ingredients. In a mixture, add the mash just before the last batch of ingredients to be fried (which will be the veg in a meat-veg combo), return all the rest to the wok, together with chillies or chilli sauce if so desired, and season with a pinch of sugar and light soy sauce. After brief tossing over intense heat to blend flavors, the dish is ready to serve.

You may vary the sauce from heavy to light. For dark, thick, rich sauce and in braised dishes, use more beans and garlic, thoroughly pulverize them, and season the sauce with both dark and light soy sauces; cover and simmer briefly to develop full flavor; at the end thicken any remaining liquid with cornstarch. For lighter, more delicate sauces, as for quick stir-fry combinations, use less and mash less vigorously in order to leave most of the beans whole.

As for what to cook with black bean sauce, it is particularly good with bell peppers—with chicken, beef, or pork; with crab; with braised stuffed eggplant; with string beans or long beans, cabbage, or asparagus.

SPRING ONIONS *Choeng* 葱

APPEARANCE: Europeans and North Americans will know these as scallions or green onions. Note that the leaves are tubular and a white bulb is present (cf. Chinese chives, *gau choi*), and that they are usually sold individually, year-round (cf. Kiangsi chives, *kiu choi*).

QUALITY: In accordance with the Cantonese belief that the bulb is the best part, select sturdy plants with long white necks. Often the smaller bulbs have a milder flavor.

COMMENTS: According to the Cantonese, although the greens may be more conspicuous, the white bulb is more valuable. Like other onions, these are classified as warming and pungent, with qualities that can stimulate and improve digestion. Unlike the larger onions, they are mild, hence seldom offensive, and welcome in a wide range of dishes, for color, flavor, and the ability to mask potentially unpleasant odours. Furthermore, spring onions are reputed to have the ability to ward off the common cold in its early stages—simply simmer a handful of *choeng* in water with a bit of mint or ginger, then go to bed while the pungency induces perspiration, thereby expelling the 'cold'.
To store spring onions, either leave whole, wrapped in a paper towel in a plastic bag, or wash, trim, chop in convenient lengths and pile in a paper-lined plastic box.

PREPARATION: Remove any dying outer leaves; wash what remains carefully, particularly at the bulb and particularly if you plan to serve them raw.

COOKING:
Western Chop leaves finely or snip with scissors; toss in salads or use as a garnish for soups, casseroles, dips, etc. Or, more simply, leave whole, dip the bulb in salt and eat as is.
Chinese Because of their attractive appearance and salubrious properties, spring onions are used with wild—and, take note, almost raw—abandon. Scatter small bits on top of soup, congee, and steamed dishes; add 1-inch lengths to stir-fry mixtures; incorporate in fried rice or fried noodles. Add, in fact, to any dish—but particularly to those mild in flavor and/or color, such as fish, bean curd, and egg dishes.

FRAGRANT NOODLES
Boil noodles in water with salt and a little oil. In a serving bowl, place finely shredded fresh ginger and chopped spring onions.
Pour a little hot oil over these, and season with soy sauce. When the noodles are cooked, drain them, rinse momentarily with cold water, and toss immediately in the warm, flavored oil.

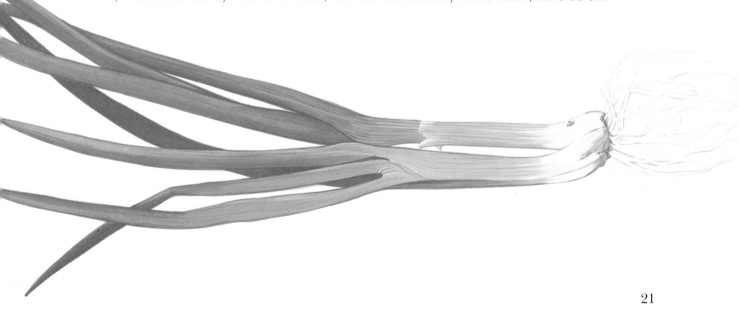

SHALLOTS *Choeng tau* 蔥頭

APPEARANCE: A diminutive member of the onion tribe, the shallot measures 3/4–1 inch in diameter. They have the group's characteristic papery husks, in a range of colors from reddish-purple to brown. In Hong Kong markets they generally appear in loose profusion, somewhere near the garlic and garlic shallots.

QUALITY: Select these as you would any onion, avoiding those with signs of shrivelling, bruises, fungus, or soft rot.

COMMENTS: This is a mild and sweet variation on the onion theme. Translation of the Chinese name accurately explains how this member fits into the family. *Choeng* are spring onions or scallions; *tau* means head; and, indeed, these are the bulbs that develop if salad onions are left in the ground to grow for two years. The French name for this sort of onion is *eschalogne*, from which come both English names, shallot and scallion.
Nutritionally, the Cantonese reckon these have the same warming effect on the stomach as spring onions, but are a bit stronger.

PREPARATION: Peel off dried outer skins and slice off roots. Leave whole for braising, or chop as desired.

COOKING:
Western The muted properties of shallots make them versatile. They may be used along the entire range of cooking methods: from serving raw in salads to sautéing with other vegetables, to braising whole in casseroles, to deep-frying. Deep-fried as tiny onion rings they make an outstanding garnish for soups, casseroles, vegetables, and salads—wherever sweet crisp onion flavor seems appropriate.
Asian Asian cooks commonly use shallots in the three following forms:
(1) Sliced and separated into rings, which are deep-fried until crisp and used to garnish curries and salads;
(2) Whole, braised with meat, poultry and/or other vegetables; and
(3) Minced finely, to be used as a subtle flavoring in cooking; Cantonese cooks, in particular, have great appreciation for the delicate flavor of shallots. In cooking chicken, for example, they maintain that the secret to making inferior frozen birds taste as good as fresh is including minced shallots in the marinade. For all mixtures and meats to be steamed with a bit of onion flavor, shallots are the onion of choice.

GARLIC SHALLOTS *Suen jee* 蒜子

APPEARANCE: These small members of the onion tribe are round, about the same size as shallots (i.e. 1/2 inch or so in diameter), and about the same color as garlic (i.e. with a white papery husk). Similarly, like a clove of garlic, but unlike shallots, they are solid rather than layered in cross-section.

QUALITY: Evaluate these as you would onions or garlic, selecting robust, firm individuals with no sign of the black powdery fungus that typically afflicts these vegetables.

COMMENTS: Botanically, these are the first year's growth of garlic seeds. They are called 'rounds' in the horticultural trade, and produce the typical cloven head of garlic when planted out.

Understandably, then, *suen jee* manifest the nutritional qualities of mature garlic (q.v.), but to a lesser degree and with a finer, sweeter, less aggressive flavor. Hence, they are a potent yet palatable, appropriate, and favored means of warming the 'coolness' of green vegetables in cooking.

PREPARATION: Peel.

COOKING:
Western Use as you would ordinary garlic, particularly in situations where the latter would overpower more delicate flavors. Garlic shallots are excellent, for example, in salad dressings, cream soups, and gentle sautés.

Chinese For the Cantonese, these are for stir-frying and braising. Where restaurant menus list vegetables 'with minced garlic', the cook is more likely to use these than cloven garlic (if available), and will use them liberally.

In general, then, use garlic shallots for stir-frying virtually any green vegetable—from water spinach, Chinese spinach and lettuce to the host of green cabbages, including broccoli. The standard procedure is to add the shallots, finely minced, to the hot oil just before the vegetables. Stir and toss, season with salt, add a bit of water to create steam, clamp the lid on, and wait until done.

Alternatively, use garlic shallots whole in braised casseroles, particularly with rich meats and seafood. Eel with braised garlic shallots, for example, is particularly popular in winter, while dried scallop with garlic shallots is famous year-round.

CORIANDER *Yuen sai* 芫茜

APPEARANCE: Fresh coriander is usually sold as small plants, 4–6 inches long, each comprising a cluster of leaves arising from a small taproot. It looks much like its cousin, parsley, but the differences are many. Note that coriander leaflets are smaller, more delicate in texture, more hemispherical in shape, always flat—and distinctly scented.

QUALITY: Choose plants with more leaflet and less leaf stalk. Leaflets should be large, sprightly, and bright green.

COMMENTS: Coriander has been in the kitchen since the heydays of Egypt, Rome, and the Six Dynasties of China. Its seeds are used in the Middle East, while the leaves are used in India (known as *hara dhania*) and Mexico (known as *cilantro*), as well as China. The etymology of the plant's name—from the Greek *koros* meaning bug—warns of the herb's ambivalent nature.

True Western parsley and coriander are botanically distinct, albeit closely related, in the same family as carrot and celery. Interestingly, both are used in their respective regions by the cooks as garnish—and by the herbalists as medicine. In the terms of Chinese medicine, coriander has 'warm, pungent, expanding' energy, with the ability to promote digestion where insufficient gastric activity, or 'cold' stomach, is the problem, and to stimulate blood circulation. Hence, it is used in cooking to harmonize two specific situations: first, to warm food of 'cold' energy, specifically fish and certain seafood (crabs, oysters, clams); second, to eliminate offensive odours of fish, pork, or beef.

Chemical analysis shows coriander leaves to be exceptionally high in virtually all vitamins and minerals; this perhaps explains its stimulating effect on digestion. The bright color of the leaves suggests an abundance of chlorophyll, which is a known purifier and cleanser of blood, breath, and tissues. In summary, then, coriander can be used to enrich your food and enliven your guests, but only in discrete amounts that do not overpower.

PREPARATION: Treat coriander gently because once it wilts it cannot be revived. For best results, store it in a plastic box or inflated plastic bag, possibly with the roots wrapped in a bit of moist paper towel. When ready to use, rinse the leaves lightly and shake them dry immediately.

COOKING:

Western Use coriander as a substitute for parsley in garnishing and seasoning, but remember its smell and flavor are stronger and potentially offensive; some people simply can't stand it. It is particularly appropriate for salads; for fish, crab, and clam dishes; and for beef soup (see below).

Chinese Hong Kong Cantonese associate fresh coriander with fish and beef as ingredients, and with steaming and boiling as methods of cooking. Hence coriander appears commonly (but not exclusively) as a garnish atop steamed fish, steamed savoury custards, and steamed minced meat mixtures, and as the final ingredient of certain types of congee, chowder, and soup.

MINCED BEEF & CORIANDER CHOWDER

1/2 lb beef, minced
3 egg whites, lightly beaten
2 tsp shredded ginger
2 tsp minced spring onions
2 tsp minced coriander
5–6 cups water or broth
2 tsp cornstarch

Season beef with salt, sugar, wine, and soy sauce for at least 15 minutes. Bring water or broth to the boil; add beef and simmer 10 minutes. Adjust seasoning. Thicken soup with cornstarch mixed to a paste with a little water. Add egg whites to the soup while stirring vigorously with a fork, in order to create fine shreds. Place ginger, onions, and coriander in bottom of tureen, or in the bottoms of bowls, and pour hot soup over. Serve.

FISH & CORIANDER SOUP

1/2 lb fresh fish fillets, chopped
3 bunches of coriander, leaves chopped finely
1–2 slices fresh ginger, crushed
2 tsp Chinese pickled melon (*cha gwa* 茶瓜)*
(Preserved duck egg, *pei daan* 皮蛋)
4–5 cups chicken stock

Shell and chop the egg. Bring stock with ginger, cucumber, and egg to the boil; simmer 5–10 minutes. Add fish and coriander; return to the simmer for about 5 minutes; when fish is cooked, adjust seasoning and serve.

*For the pickled melon you may substitute salted-fresh cucumber. In this case, peel the cucumber, seed, chop in small matchsticks, sprinkle lightly with (coarse) salt and let rest. After 10–20 minutes, rinse, squeeze, and add to the broth with a pinch of sugar and a dash of vinegar.

CHILLI PEPPERS *Laat jiu* 辣椒

APPEARANCE: Generally, small size and elongated shape distinguish chillies from sweet peppers, but beware the fiery small, round, green ones do exist.

QUALITY: Select firm, unblemished peppers, preferably with stems. Hotness differs more with variety than with color, although green ones tend to be hotter than red because the fruits sweeten as they ripen.

COMMENTS: Vegetable peppers (as opposed to peppercorns) are a relatively recent addition to the cuisines of both Europe and Asia, having emigrated from South America via Columbus, first to Europe and then further eastward. Today they are a staple in many provinces of China. One cook reports that 'Hunan people can live without meat but [not] without hot pepper,' and that every home garden has a plant or two.

The Cantonese, however, take a somewhat dimmer view of this vegetable/condiment. They consider chillies to be one of the few foods that is downright 'hot'—not just 'warm'—and consume them with commensurate wariness. In small amounts, chillies are respected as an excellent general stimulant (of the appetite, nerves, blood circulation, perspiration), hence particularly appropriate to combat the stagnating heat, dampness, and lethargy of summer. Indeed, hot food is ironically appropriate for hot climates because it discourages over-eating by quickly satisfying the stomach and because it cools the body by encouraging blood to rush to the skin's surface (away from the chilli, as it were). Nevertheless, the Cantonese advise anyone with the slightest sign of heat in the body, e.g. inflammation of any tissue, internal or external, to avoid chillies at all cost.

PREPARATION: Wash. Before continuing, determine how hot your chillies are. First touch the tip of your tongue to the pepper, and wait; if after one minute a burning sensation develops, you've got a Very Hot one. If you feel nothing, nibble a tiny piece; thereafter, you can label your pepper Medium or Mild. Use quantities accordingly.

For further preparation, slit the chilli(es) lengthwise; remove and discard the seeds, which are reputed to be hotter than the flesh. Chop as desired—and immediately thereafter wash knife, chopping board and hands before preparing other food.

COOKING: Chillies are indispensable to many cuisines, but not traditional Cantonese home cooking. Nevertheless, the fresh item is perennial in Hong Kong markets, and commercial chilli sauces are standard condiments in both homes and restaurants—particularly for noodles, dumplings, fish balls, bean curd, and deep-fried items.

CHINESE FLOWERING CABBAGE *Choi sum* 菜心

APPEARANCE: Distinguish this vegetable—particularly from its cousin Chinese kale—by its yellow flowers, stems that are uniform in diameter and faintly grooved from tip to base, and bright green color.

QUALITY: The more easily your fingernail can pierce the base of the stem the more tender it is. Like all cabbages, this is sweeter and more tender when grown during colder weather.

COMMENTS: Some people will argue that this is the best of the Chinese cabbages. Stems are uniform in size (hence cook evenly) and need not be peeled; leaves are tender; whole stalks cook quickly; the taste is pleasant—quite mild for a cabbage, and its bright color is attractive. In Hong Kong, this is undoubtedly the most common leafy vegetable. Virtually year-round it graces bowls of noodles in simple foodstalls and garnishes platters at restaurant banquets, or appears as simply a side dish on its own. In other words, *choi sum* is considered to be an almost neutral vegetable—the perfect plain side dish—with no nutritional excesses nor deficiencies requiring compensation. Although mild, *choi sum* does have slightly 'cooling', pungent tendencies common to all cabbages; hence, in cooking it benefits from a clove of garlic or slice of ginger for 'warmth', with a pinch of sugar and dressing of oil to tame the pungency.

PREPARATION: Soak in water briefly to remove dirt, particularly at the bases of leaf blades. For Cantonese cooking leave whole, if less than 8 inches or so long.

COOKING:
Western Prepare as for tender broccoli; that is, boil or steam briefly, drain, and season with salt, pepper, butter, or hollandaise sauce. Or beat together soy sauce and cold-pressed oil and pour over the hot, cooked, drained vegetable.
Chinese The simplest approach is to parboil it in salted water with a dash of oil (or soup stock); drain. Then add to noodles in soup; or serve alone, as a side dish, possibly doused with oyster sauce; or mound in the centre of a dish and cover with braised mixtures (example below); or arrange as a border on platters of meat, bean curd, or other green-less courses. Alternatively, stir-fry it with garlic, without or with virtually any meat or fish.

Winter Mushrooms and cabbage

Winter mushrooms (*doeng gwu* 冬菇) preferably small whole ones, soaked
Choi sum, washed
Ginger
Oyster sauce

Parboil the cabbage until just tender; while still bright green, drain; arrange on a serving dish. Stir-fry the mushrooms in oil with a slice of ginger; add the liquid in which the mushrooms soaked, and water or chicken stock to cover the mushrooms about three-quarters. Cover and simmer 4—5 minutes. Season with oyster sauce, thicken with cornstarch if necessary, and pour mushrooms-cum-sauce over the cooked vegetable.

Braised Bean Curd and Cabbage

Fresh bean curd
Choi sum, washed
Garlic
Ginger
Soy sauce

Parboil the cabbage until just tender; drain. Rinse the bean curd; cut large cubes in half horizontally, then each half into two or four pieces. In a little oil, sauté a crushed clove or two of garlic; discard the garlic, then add the cubes of bean curd. Fry—rather quickly over medium–high heat—until each surface has a light brown crust. Add a crushed slice of ginger, season with soy sauce (and chilli if desired), add a little water, cover, and braise 3–4 minutes to blend flavors. Uncover; thicken the sauce with cornstarch. You may then either return the ch*oi sum* to the pan to cook briefly with the bean curd, or simply pour the bean curd over the *choi sum* on the serving platter.

CHINESE WHITE CABBAGE *Baak choi* 白菜

APPEARANCE: Of the many varieties of *baak choi* (also spelled 'bok choy'), all can generally be identified (1) by their strikingly two-tone leaves: ivory-white leaf stalks topped by dark green leaves; and (2) by their compressed, clustering growth form.

There are two outstanding exceptions to these rules, both from Shanghai. The first is actually known as 'Shanghai *baak choi*', although exported produce comes principally from Taiwan these days. It has the typical clustered form, but its leaves and stalks are uniformly light green. The second is called Chinese flat cabbage or *tai gu choi*. It has the bicoloured leaves but in a different shape (see page 33).

QUALITY: The most reliable measure of tenderness—and flavor—is the width of the base of the oldest leaf: the wider it is relative to the length of the leaf, the more tender is the vegetable. Overall plant size is not necessarily an indicator of tenderness, although the smallest clusters, which measure about 3 inches in both height and width, are indeed the choicest.

COMMENTS: Chinese white cabbage is known to have been grown in China since the fifth century AD, and in Europe since the mid-18th century. During that time four major subgroups have emerged: the vegetable pictured here; the white flowering cabbage (q.v.); the flat cabbage (q.v.); and rapeseed (*yau choi*) grown for its seeds, which yield oil for cooking and lighting. 'Canola oil' is a variety of rapeseed oil custom-designed by plant breeders for higher nutrition and easier digestion.

If ever there was a vegetable for all seasons, this is it. The leaf stalks are succulent, while the leaves are tender; both have a mild version of cabbage flavor that can stand alone or blend amicably with other savoury tastes in a wide range of culinary delights. It can be eaten fresh, dried, salted, or preserved, in soups, casseroles, or stir-fry dishes; Americans even eat it raw.

According to Chinese nutritional theory, *baak choi* falls on the cool side of neutral. It is said to aid digestion, with the ability to reduce heat in three of the major internal organs (i.e. lungs, stomach, liver). This is valuable for those who are 'overheated', but not for those with weak digestion. Hence, in most cases, garlic is added when stir-frying, and ginger when boiling or braising it in order to guarantee balance.

PREPARATION: With smaller bunches, leave whole. With larger ones, separate leaves. In either case, wash well to remove dirt trapped between stem and leaf bases. Drain. (N.B. Leaves less than about 6 inches long are left whole, even if diners have to chew through them in several bites.)

Like lettuce and spinach, this cabbage is mostly water. Thus it loses at least 50 per cent of its volume as it cooks, so wash up a fair amount in anticipation of shrinkage.

COOKING:

Western Prepare this as you would head cabbage or spinach. If very fresh and tender, use in salad. If not, boil, steam, or sauté. It will benefit from something aromatic (e.g. ginger, garlic, caraway seeds), something sweet (e.g. slices of carrot, pinch of sugar), and something rich (e.g. butter or bacon) in the cooking.

Chinese The Cantonese consider this cabbage equally suitable for soup, casserole, or stir-fry. When stir-frying or braising, add a crushed clove of garlic to the oil first. Combine it with beef, chicken, or pork; with Cantonese roast pork (*cha siu* 叉燒); with winter mushrooms and carrots; with wood ear mushrooms (*wun yee* 云耳), egg, and mung bean vermicelli (*fun see* 粉絲). Or simply parboil, drain, and serve doused with oyster sauce.

When making soup, an equally wide range of supplementary ingredients can help flavor the broth—but ginger is a must. One traditional tonic soup calls for fresh and dried *baak choi*, a few bitter almonds, a few dried Peking dates (*mut jo* 蜜棗), and a cleaned pig's lung. Other potential soup combinations are *baak choi* with: pork, meat or bones, and winter melon; chicken giblets and Chinese red dates (*hoeng jo* 紅棗); ham and chicken's feet. Alternatively, a vegetarian recipe is outlined below. In all cases, allow at least an hour of gentle simmering to mellow the vegetable and develop the soup's full flavor.

CABBAGE & CASHEW SOUP
1/4 cup raw cashew nuts
2 potatoes
3 small tomatoes
Baak choi
Ginger, one slice, crushed

Use approximately three times as much *baak choi* as everything else; leave leaves whole. Combine all—except the *choi*—in a soup pot with water to cover generously. Add a teaspoon of oil. Bring to the boil, add the *choi*, then simmer gently until liquid is reduced by 1/3 and broth is well flavored. Season with salt and pepper, and serve.

PEKING CABBAGE *Wong nga baak* 黃芽白

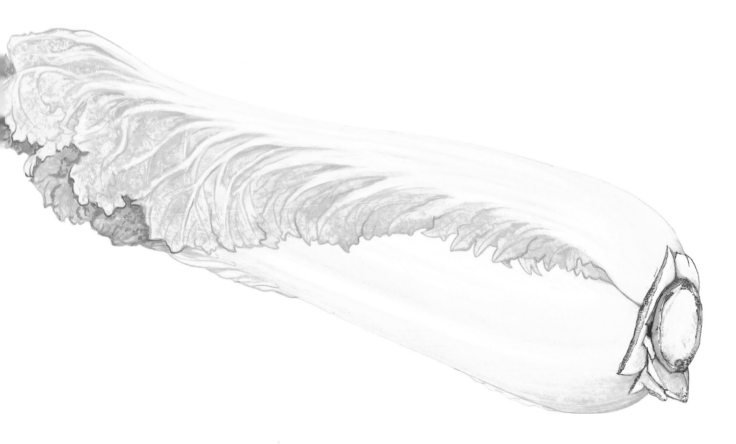

APPEARANCE: A compact barrel shape, pale color, and broadly ribbed leaf stalks with crinkled leaves characterize this vegetable. It comes in two styles: long and narrow (12–18 x 3–4 inches diameter, as illustrated); and short and stout (up to 12 inches long and more than 5 inches in diameter).

QUALITY: Select heavy, compact heads with whole leaves. Both styles taste—and generally cost—the same. Those from Tientsin are considered the best; those slightly wilted are considered sweeter; white heads and leaves are more tender than green.

COMMENTS: Also known as Peking, Shantung, or Tientsin nappa, as well as celery cabbage, *chou de Chine* and *pe-tsai*, this vegetable's aliases attest to its global popularity. Its mild cabbage taste mellows as it cooks, blending with and subtly enhancing the flavors of foods it accompanies. The texture is generally tender and succulent, whether stir-fried, braised, or pickled.

Like common head cabbage, this keeps well. In the countryside, housewives store the long narrow variety by hanging, and they swear it sweetens as it wilts.

PREPARATION: Wash; chop as desired. When using the whole head, simply chop through from tip to base, rather than first separating leaves.

COOKING:
Western Peking cabbage can be eaten raw; and its sweetness, mild pungency, and tender texture make it far more suitable for the purpose than ordinary head cabbage. The heart is particularly nice for salad. To serve it cooked, boil, steam, or braise; blanch and roll a stuffing in individual leaves; or bake in a cream sauce *au gratin*.

Chinese The Chinese of all provinces use this versatile cabbage in a wide and colorful spectrum of dishes. It is braised in casseroles and hotpots; stir-fried with other vegetables and/or meats and/or noodles; included in fillings for spring rolls or dumplings; and salted and pickled. Its ability to absorb flavors and its pleasant texture make it equally compatible with rich tastes (such as beneath beef in oyster sauce) or with delicate ones (such as fish and bean curd), with salty ones (such as ham) or with sweet ones (such as chestnuts). Blanched leaves may be rolled with a filling (such as mashed fresh shrimp or minced pork), and steamed or braised.

Gentle braising generally suits this vegetable better than aggressive stir-frying; and it benefits from stimulation, as in the addition of garlic at the start or ginger later in the cooking process. The recommended procedure is to begin cooking on high heat, season the veg, then cover the pot and reduce the heat, gently braising the contents to perfection.

PEKING CASSEROLE
1–2 small bamboo shoots
Gluten, either fresh (*meen gun* 麵筋) or deep-fried (*saang gun* 生筋), in quantities to taste
5–10 winter mushrooms (*doeng gwu* 冬菇), soaked
2–3 cups Peking cabbage, washed, sliced diagonally
Ginger, 1–2 slices, crushed

If using fresh bamboo shoots, prepare them by peeling and parboiling; drain; slice in bite-size rectangles. If using fresh gluten, slice it in 1/4-inch slabs, then sauté in oil until lightly browned on both sides. If using deep-fried gluten puffs, rinse them in boiling water to remove excess oil.

In large braising pot, sauté mushrooms in oil over medium heat until the fragrance of cooking mushrooms becomes apparent. Add ginger, gluten, and water (including mushroom-soaking liquid) to a depth of 1/4 of the ingredients. Bring to the boil; add cabbage; season with a little salt, sugar, and soy sauce. Cover and braise gently, approximately half an hour.

RAINBOW FRIED NOODLES
Egg noodles (or spaghetti)
Winter mushrooms (*doeng gwu* 冬菇), soaked
Carrot
Peking cabbage
Wood ear mushrooms (*wun yee* 云耳), soaked
Mung bean sprouts
Chinese white cabbage (*baak choi* 白菜)

Cook noodles in boiling salted water; drain; toss with a bit of oil to keep strands separate.

Chop winter mushrooms and carrot in matchstick-type pieces; chop Peking cabbage similarly but in larger pieces. Pick over soaked wood ear mushrooms to remove bits of wood and other debris.

To cook, in wok fry mushrooms (seasoned with soy sauce) until fragrant. Add carrot, Peking cabbage, and wood ear mushrooms with a little liquid; cover and braise about 3 minutes to cook through. Uncover, add sprouts and *baak choi*; toss again. As these begin to cook, add noodles. Integrate all ingredients by lifting with two implements (e.g. ladles, chopsticks, wooden spoons), one in each hand, gently teasing apart the noodles and tossing them with the vegetables. When satisfactorily homogenous, serve.

CHINESE FLAT CABBAGE *Tai gu choi* 太古菜

APPEARANCE: This cabbage grows like a flat, round plate or saucer, only a few inches tall but 5–14 inches in diameter. The leafstalks have the familiar ivory color of Chinese white cabbage, *baak choi*.

QUALITY: Smaller plants with many young leaves clustered tightly at the centre are the best.

GENERAL COMMENTS: Although this is simply a form of ordinary Chinese white cabbage, *baak choi*, it is one of the most ingenious plant varieties ever discovered or devised. Growing so close to the ground, it can easily be protected from killing frost, and hence survive for harvesting well after everything else has shrivelled up and died.

Not surprisingly, this has the same flavor and same nutritional attributes of *baak choi*, but is a bit tougher in texture.

PREPARATION: Wash, giving special attention to the leaf bases. For cooking, cut it up like a pie (i.e. into radial sections), rather than separating the leaves.

COOKING: Ordinarily, this is stir-fried or braised, but is certainly suitable for all the other multifarious methods applied to its versatile cousin. Using a clove or two of garlic in cooking it is recommended.

CHINESE KALE   *Gai laan*   芥蘭

APPEARANCE: Distinguish this from other cabbages by its white flowers, the white haze on its vaguely blue-green leaves, and its overall stoutness. Unlike Chinese flowering cabbage, *choi sum*, this vegetable has stems which are smooth, not grooved, and which can reach 1/2–1 inch in diameter.

QUALITY: Select plants with unblemished leaves, more flowers in bud than in bloom, and with stalks either very thin (hence no need to peel) or very thick (hence with a large pith, which is a crisp, sweet delicacy).

COMMENTS: This is less common than either *choi sum* or *baak choi*, and more seasonal, appearing only during the colder months. Robust both in flavor and texture, it is a bit bitter, a bit pungent, and—sometimes, especially the older leaves—a bit tough. The mild, crisp pith of the stem, however, offers sweet compensation for all of these shortcomings.
Likewise, in terms of nutrition, *gai laan* is considered more cooling and harsh to the stomach than the other members of the Chinese cabbage family (except, perhaps, mustard cabbage). The Cantonese turn this to advantage by cooking it with rich sauces, typically oyster or *sadeh* sauce (see below), or with seafood.

PREPARATION: Soak briefly in water to cleanse. Leave whole for serving Chinese style. Otherwise, remove leaves and chop coarsely, possibly discarding the tough middle rib, especially of older leaves. With larger stems, peel the lower portions and chop what remains into pieces of uniform size for even cooking.

COOKING:

Western Prepare as you would broccoli. Steam or boil it, chopped or as whole stalks, in a minimum of water; drain, season with salt, pepper and butter, or with a cheese or hollandaise sauce.

Chinese Stir-frying is the preferred method for preparing this vegetable, although it is also served parboiled with oyster sauce. Stir-fry it alone, with meat, or with mushrooms; add a dash of cooking wine and a pinch of sugar when the vegetable is half-cooked to tenderize and balance flavors. The following Chiu Chow (Swatow) dish is one of the most popular forms of serving *gai laan* in Hong Kong, and brings three similarly outspoken ingredients happily together.

SADEH BEEF & GAI LAAN

Gai laan
Beef, cut across the grain in thin slices and marinated
Garlic, crushed
Sadeh sauce* (沙爹醬)
(Chilli, chopped or sauce)

Mix a hefty spoonful of the *sadeh* sauce with an equal amount of water to make a thick sauce, which you will be able to pour into the wok later. Stir-fry the beef and remove. Stir-fry the *gai laan*, beginning with the garlic. When it is almost cooked, add your slightly-diluted *sadeh* sauce and the cooked beef (and the chilli if desired). Continue to toss until flavors have blended, ingredients are mixed, and the sauce lightly and evenly coats everything; serve.

*'*Sadeh* sauce' (沙爹醬) is a dark brown, mildly spicy paste sold in jars. This is a Chinese concoction, decidedly different from and not to be confused with Indonesian 'satay sauce'. Substitute dark soy sauce, or light soy sauce.

MUSTARD CABBAGES *Gai choi* 芥菜

APPEARANCE: A multitude of mustard cabbages reach Chinese markets. Three characteristics can be used to identify them all: an overall pale green color; thin-textured leaves with irregular edges; and stemless form (with all leaves attached at the base of the stem). Two forms are illustrated here:

Swatow Mustard Cabbage (*Dai gai choi* 大芥菜): Like a head of lettuce in size and shape, but the leaves are all stalk and much stouter.

Bamboo Mustard Cabbage (*Jook gai choi* 竹芥菜): Long and thin, this differs from *choi sum* in the notched leaf edges and blades extending nearly to the stem.

QUALITY: For all, select plants with large, well-formed leaf midribs because this is considered the best part for eating. Pale color suggests tenderness.

COMMENTS: Mustard cabbage has nourished Chinese people and their livestock since before the beginning of recorded agricultural history. Some of the crop is eaten fresh, but most is pickled: salted according to the same principles by which the Germans make sauerkraut from head cabbage. Different salting methods and different varieties of cabbage create a range of Chinese sauerkrauts,

from the whole-headed salt-sour cabbage (*haam suen choi* 鹹酸菜) of Swatow to the preserved snow cabbage (*suet lui hoeng* 雪裏紅) of Shanghai.

The fact that most mustard cabbages become pickle expresses the Chinese opinion that it's not too good for you fresh. Indeed, it comprises one of the most bitter members of the cabbage clan, and digesting its constituents can be a challenge to the stomach. Hence, mustard cabbage is particularly valued for its therapeutic uses, e.g. in clearing the body of flu; otherwise it requires skillful cooking—or fermenting—for daily consumption.

PREPARATION: Wash heads well, particularly at the leaf bases. For making soup with *dai gai choi*, chop whole head crosswise in slices or chunks. For the more bitter types, parboil or blanch before further cooking or serving.

COOKING:
Western Sweetness in the seasoning and oil in the cooking complement it well. Hence, sauté with garlic in bacon drippings; or in butter with dill or caraway seeds; or toss with sour cream and chives.

Chinese For Cantonese, fresh *dai gai choi* (the head type) is strictly soup material. As with other cabbages, bring water to a rolling boil before adding the vegetable; simmer at least one hour. To flavor the broth, use pork bones, pork shin, or barbecued roast duck; and/or add a salted duck egg (*haam daan*) at the end.

To prepare a side dish from the other mustard cabbages, blanch and drain. Then stir-fry with garlic, with garlic and fermented black beans, with meat or seafood, or simply dress with oyster sauce.

FLU-FIGHTING SOUP
Fresh mustard cabbage, washed, chopped coarsely
Bean curd
Slices of fresh fish

Bring water to the boil. Add the cabbage. Simmer 10–15 minutes. Add the bean curd, then the fish. When all is cooked, serve immediately.

HEAD CABBAGE   *Yeh choi* 椰菜

APPEARANCE: This vegetable is a solid, yellow-white ball of overlapping, tightly clasping leaves; diameters vary from 6 to 12 inches.

QUALITY: Heads should be heavy and compact; particularly look for and avoid those with signs of soft rot at the stem. Green leaves are more nutritious but white ones are more tender.

COMMENTS: This cabbage originated in Europe and has only relatively recently joined its Asian relatives. While traditional Chinese cooks still consider it foreigners' food, younger chefs have found it a place in modern, home cuisine. Availability and competitive price are strong persuasion. The Cantonese name *yeh choi* translates as 'coconut vegetable' and presumably refers both to its appearance and to the mild, nutty crunch of the leaves eaten raw or lightly cooked.

PREPARATION: Wash. Tear individual leaves into bite-sized pieces, or slice a section from the entire head.

COOKING:
Western The extensive repertoire of Western recipes for cabbage reflects its easy and historically lengthy culture. Serve it raw, cooked, or pickled; baked, braised, boiled, sautéed, creamed, or stuffed.
Chinese Stir-frying is an excellent method of cooking cabbage because it brings out maximum sweetness with a minimum of the unpleasant pungency in the smell and taste of overcooked cabbage. Stir-fry it on its own, seasoned only with salt; or with shredded beef or pork. Alternatively, use it like Peking cabbage in the following casserole:

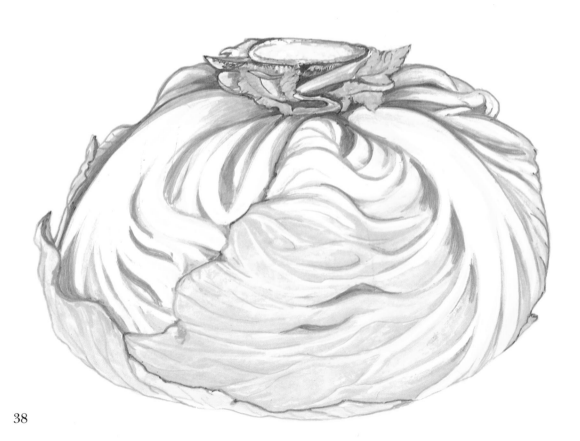

CABBAGE, SHRIMP & VERMICELLI

1 tsp dried shrimp (*ha mai* 蝦米)
1 handful mung bean vermicelli (*fun see* 粉絲)
3–4 cups coarsely shredded or torn cabbage
1 slice fresh ginger, crushed

With kitchen scissors or a knife, cut the wet vermicelli into 4–5-inch lengths for easier eating later; drain it. Heat oil in wok, fry shrimp a minute or two, then add cabbage and ginger. Toss vigorously and season with salt, a pinch of sugar, and a dash of wine. Add water to a depth of 1/4 inch or so, then distribute vermicelli over top. Cover and cook over rather high heat so as to braise the cabbage and steam-cook the vermicelli. When virtually done, remove lid, toss, and continue to cook to reduce any liquid remaining. Adjust seasoning, and serve.

SIMPLE AND SPICY SHANGHAI CABBAGE

Head cabbage
Green peppers
Red peppers
Pressed bean curd
Spring onions
Garlic
Ginger
Soy sauce (preferably a mixture of dark and light)
Chilli sauce (preferably the Shanghai broad bean chilli sauce) known as *dau baan laat
    jeung*)

Tear the cabbage into bite-sized bits; chop the green and red peppers similarly. Chop the pressed bean curd into 1/2" cubes. In hot oil in the wok, first stir-fry the bean curd until it is golden and crusty on most of its sides; remove. Again heat oil in the wok: add, in quick succession, a crushed clove or two of garlic, one or two slices of crushed ginger, the cabbage, peppers, and spring onions. Toss until wilted. Season with the soy sauces (the dark sauce will give the rich color, characteristic of Shanghai dishes), a dab of chilli sauce, and just enough water to allow the mixture to braise; cover; reduce heat and simmer until the vegetables are cooked but still crisp. Uncover. The water should have evapourated or been absorbed into sauce; if not, thicken what remains with some cornstarch, cook another 2–3 minutes, then serve.

WATERCRESS   *Sai yeung choi* 西洋菜

APPEARANCE: In Hong Kong markets this vegetable appears in great heaps—and only during the winter. Identify it by the red-purple tint and irregular shape of its small leaflets. Note, too, the small white roots often found growing at the bases of leaves along the lower stems.

QUALITY: Tender green tips are best; buy as little of the thick, tough lower stems as possible.

COMMENTS: Apparently Hong Kong was responsible for introducing this plant to China around the turn of the 20th century. Easy to grow and of a familiar cabbage flavor, it has since joined the crowd of common market and family dinner-table vegetables.

Watercress resembles its relatives, the mustards, more than its cousins, the leafy cabbages. Raw shoots are peppery sharp with a sinus-clearing pungency. 'Too cool!' say the Cantonese, who rarely eat any vegetable raw, much less this one grown in muddy water, and instead boil the living daylights out of it in soup. With long boiling, watercress turns olive-green, limp, and stringy while yielding a rich broth. Such soup is believed to clear phlegm from the respiratory system and to cleanse and cool the blood, hence benefiting every cell in the body.

PREPARATION: Soak in water and wash carefully. Discard yellowing lower leaves and toughest lower inches of stems.

COOKING:

Western Western cooks add this green to salads, include it in sandwiches (especially with cream cheese), and purée it to make a refreshing soup.

Chinese The Cantonese concede that stir-frying this green is possible, but most commonly they boil it in some variation of the following winter specialty. Almonds are added to 'lubricate' the lungs; the sweetness of the dates counterbalances the bitter component in the cress's flavor, while the tangerine peel is believed to harmonize the entire concoction for better absorption by the body. For best flavor, always bring the water to a rolling boil before adding the watercress.

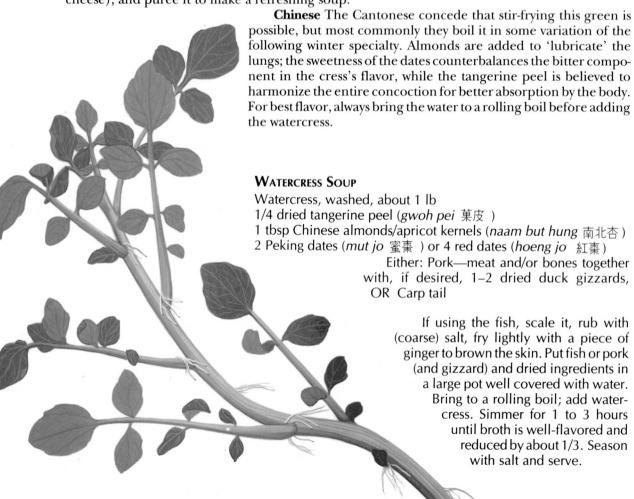

WATERCRESS SOUP
Watercress, washed, about 1 lb
1/4 dried tangerine peel (*gwoh pei* 菓皮)
1 tbsp Chinese almonds/apricot kernels (*naam but hung* 南北杏)
2 Peking dates (*mut jo* 蜜棗) or 4 red dates (*hoeng jo* 紅棗)
　　　Either: Pork—meat and/or bones together with, if desired, 1–2 dried duck gizzards, OR Carp tail

If using the fish, scale it, rub with (coarse) salt, fry lightly with a piece of ginger to brown the skin. Put fish or pork (and gizzard) and dried ingredients in a large pot well covered with water. Bring to a rolling boil; add watercress. Simmer for 1 to 3 hours until broth is well-flavored and reduced by about 1/3. Season with salt and serve.

KOHLRABI *Gai laan tau* 芥蘭頭

APPEARANCE: Botanically this vegetable is a swollen stem. It is as hard as a root, 2–4 inches in diameter, light green or purplish-red on the outside, always white inside, with or without leaves, but always with knobby leaf bases scattered over the surface.

QUALITY: Choose those that are solid, clear-skinned, and small. Those smaller than a tennis ball probably don't need peeling; those larger than 4–5 inches in diameter (i.e. old) can be woody. Skin color (green or red) seems unrelated to eating quality.

COMMENTS: The flesh of kohlrabi is white, tenderly crisp, and sweetly, mildly pungent. It may be eaten raw or cooked.

Kohlrabi, cauliflower, and common head cabbage are all relatively recent introductions to Asia; they are also all varieties of a single species, and hence have similar nutritional profiles. As the name, *gai laan tau*, indicates, the Cantonese associate kohlrabi with their kale (*gai laan*). The pith of the latter is the choicest part of the vegetable, and kohlrabi resembles it exactly in both flavor and texture. A bit of 'warmth'—from garlic and/or something sweet, such as a pinch of sugar, sauce, a sweet veg—is all that the Cantonese use in cooking to harmonize its cabbage-family characteristics.

PREPARATION: Remove leaves and leaf stalks; reserve for soup. If you intend to parboil it, do that before you peel it in order to retain the maximum nutrients and flavor. For other purposes, peel first. In either case, chop as desired; this is a potentially creative task as the peeled vegetable is uniform in color and texture.

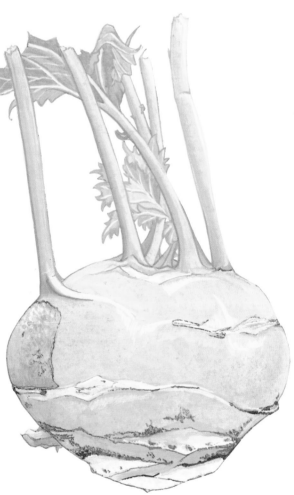

COOKING:

Western To serve raw, slice in sticks, then nibble, dip, or toss in salads. To serve cooked, parboil until almost tender, then slice and sauté, cream, and bake *au gratin*. Alternatively, boil until soft, purée for soup and flavor with dill, caraway or cumin, with sweet or sour cream.

Chinese Like the Chinese radish, kohlrabi may be braised or stewed with meat. Like bamboo shoots, it may be included in mixed vegetable dishes for contrast in color and texture. But more typically, the Cantonese stir-fry it with tender cuts of meat, or parboil and serve it, plain, under a highly flavored meat sauce. As with *gai laan*, beef is the meat of choice for combinations.

For recipes, use those described for Oriental radish (see p 118). Or the following:

OYSTER BEEF & KOHLRABI

Kohlrabi
Tender beef, shredded and seasoned
Oyster sauce, approximately 2–3 tbsp per cup of beef
Clove(s) of garlic, crushed

Peel and chop kohlrabi into large matchsticks.
Heat wok; add oil; stir-fry kohlrabi, seasoned with salt, until almost cooked; remove. Again heat wok, add oil, then garlic; when fragrant, remove; add beef. Stir and toss until almost cooked. Return the kohlrabi, and then add oyster sauce. Continue to stir and toss this combination, uncovered, over fairly high heat until flavors are blended and sauce reduced.

KOHLRABI IN CONCERT

Kohlrabi
Green and red bell peppers
Garlic
If desired: Fermented black beans (*dau see* 豆豉)
            Chilli

Crush the garlic; slice peppers in strips. Heat wok; add oil, then garlic (black beans and/or chilli). When fragrant, add kohlrabi; season with salt (or soy sauce) and a pinch of sugar. Cook over medium heat until almost done. Then raise heat very high and add peppers. Stir and toss until you detect the fragrance of cooked peppers. Add just enough water to create a cloud of steam and clamp on the lid. Continue to cook but only briefly; uncover, toss, adjust seasoning, and serve.

GARLIC CHIVES   *Gau choi* 韮菜

APPEARANCE: These are long, flat green leaves, about 1/4 inch wide, reminiscent of a green onion but always sold as leaves only, never with a bulb.

QUALITY: Uniformly dark green leaves are good; often the shorter they are, the younger and thus the more tender and mild in taste.

COMMENTS: *Gau choi* has a stronger taste and a tougher, more fibrous texture than either spring onions or true chives. Its flat, rather than tubular, leaves indicate that it belongs to the garlic clan of the onion family; even so, 'chives' is an appropriate epithet because Southeast Asians use it in the same way Westerners use chives.

Its dark green color suggests a high iron content; its ties with garlic suggest an affinity with the blood. Theories are confirmed in the Cantonese belief that eating this will invigorate blood and energy circulation and improve weak digestion. Such therapeutic virtues make chewing it worthwhile.

PREPARATION: Wash and air- or blot-dry with a towel. Store as for spring onions, i.e. preferably wrapped in a towel in a plastic bag. Without bulbs these will not keep as well as spring onions, so plan to use them within a day or two.

COOKING:

Western Chop finely in view of their tough texture, and use sparingly in deference to their stronger taste. Otherwise use in the same way as scallions or chives, in salads, soups, omelettes, dips, herb butters, etc.

Chinese Traditional Cantonese cooks serve *gau choi* simmered in a little broth with squares of coagulated pig's blood. (These squares, sold from tubs of water in market or meat stalls, have the color of cooked liver, the texture of bean curd, and surprisingly little taste.)

Northern Chinese cooks use it as a filling for pan-fried and steamed dumplings.

Alternatively, it is parboiled and served alone as a side dish, or stir-fried with slices of meat, or braised as described below.

BO JAI CHOI
Bean curd
Winter mushrooms, soaked
Gau choi, cut in 2-inch lengths
Ginger

In braising pot, fry mushrooms until fragrant; remove. Brown bean curd on all sides. Return mushrooms with a slice or two of ginger and the *gau choi*; stir to mix. Add enough water or light stock to braise; season with salt and white (or chilli) pepper; cover and simmer gently 10–15 minutes. Adjust seasoning; sauce with cornstarch if desired, drizzle with a bit of sesame thicken oil for fragrance and sheen; serve.

BLANCHED GARLIC CHIVES   *Gau wong* 韮黃

APPEARANCE: These are garlic chives (*gau choi*) that have been grown in the dark. They appear in the market in mounds of limp, yellowed, flat leaves, about 1/4 inch wide and 10–12 inches long—usually next to green mounds of *gau choi*.

QUALITY: Select only fresh leaves with no visible sign or smell of decay.

COMMENTS: The blanching process—i.e. growing the plants in the dark, traditionally under woven straw cylinders—results in weak, languishing plants. In the context of the dinner table this means tender; in the context of the refrigerator it means a short, 1–2-day shelf life. In the context of Chinese nutrition, it means they lack some of the effects on the blood for which *gau choi* is noted but can still stimulate digestion.

PREPARATION: Just before use, rinse in water, drain, and/or shake dry. Otherwise store them wrapped in a paper or cloth towel in the fridge.

COOKING:
Western Use as you would chives, but with more discretion in deference to its stronger, garlic flavor. Toss in salads, beat into omelettes, sprinkle on soups, or incorporate in simple pasta dishes.
Chinese *Gau wong* is a cosmetic vegetable, used in lightly cooked dishes where the taste but not the greenness of *gau choi* is desired. By custom, it is combined with noodles, either in soup or fried, and included in fillings for spring rolls and wonton. It is equally suitable for stir-fry mixtures, particularly with other pale ingredients such as bean sprouts and Peking cabbage.

FLOWERING GARLIC CHIVES *Gau choi fa* 韭菜花 ; *Gau choi sum* 韭菜心

APPEARANCE: As the name explains, this vegetable is the flower (*fa*) of garlic chives (*gau choi*). Identify it in the market as simple, smooth, leafless, green stems 8–10 inches long, about as thick as a ballpoint pen refill, with a single conical bud at the tip of each. (Flowering garlic shoots, *suen sum* 蒜心 , are thicker, about the diameter of a pencil.)

QUALITY: The smaller, harder and tighter the flower head, the younger the stalk and the more tender it is likely to be. Those with open flowers are considered too old to eat.

COMMENTS: Like spring onions and garlic chives, *gau choi fa* have the basic onion pungency. The stalks are thin and rather stiff, yet tender and mildly flavored. Cooked, they retain texture and probably color better than spring onions. Like *gau choi*, they are considered a warming stimulant for blood and energy—less powerful in effect but also less of a challenge to chew.

PREPARATION: Wash; store wrapped in a towel in the fridge. Some cooks advocate removing the flower buds; others—indifferent—leave them on; still others consider the buds the best part. Suit yourself.

COOKING:
Western Mince. Toss in salads, beat into omelettes, sprinkle on soup, mix in dips—in other words, use wherever you crave a dash of color and onion flavor, as a general substitute for scallions or spring onions.
Chinese The Cantonese usually chop this green in 1 1/2–2-inch lengths and stir-fry it, particularly with beef. It is also stir-fried on its own and served as a side dish with seafood, or braised with bean curd. The people of Shantung pickle the flower heads in vinegar as a delicacy.

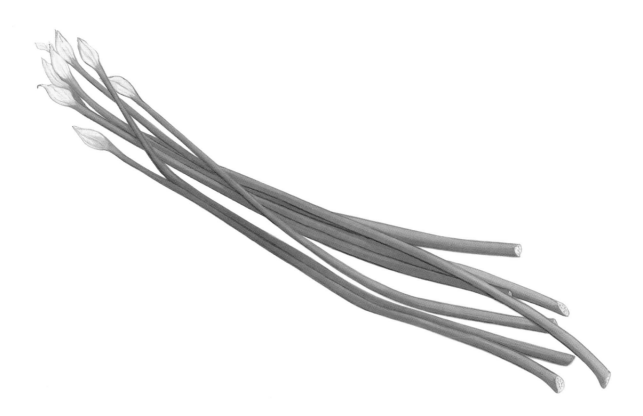

KIANGSI SCALLIONS *Kiu choi* 蕎菜

APPEARANCE: With white bulb and green leaves, these could be mistaken for spring onions or true scallions (*choeng*). The differences are: these are finer, i.e. smaller in diameter; they are invariably sold in clusters, never as individuals; and they are available only in the spring.

QUALITY: Select those with the most green leaves per plant.

COMMENTS: Sweeter and more tender than scallions, this vegetable is as close as any Asian onion comes to Western 'chives'.

PREPARATION: Wash well. Remove dead and yellowing leaves; chop them off at the neck; discard the whites and reserve the greens for cooking.

COOKING:
Western Use as you would chives, raw or cooked briefly, as garnish or ingredient.
Chinese Limited season seems to mean a limited cooking repertoire. One recipe seems to suffice for Hong Kong Cantonese: they stir-fry this vegetable with beef and peapods.

LEEKS *Dai suen* 大蒜

APPEARANCE: With a white bulb at one end and green shoots at the other, this must be a sort of onion; its large size suggests leek. Indeed it is. Distinguish it from another, similarly large, onion, the *dai choeng* (大葱)—literally 'big spring onion'—by shape and by leaves. The neck of this usually swells slightly at the base, while the neck of *dai choeng* is uniformly cylindrical; the leaves of this are flat, while those of *choeng* are tubular.

QUALITY: Ignore the green leaves; choose individuals with as large, full, white, and fresh a neck as possible as this is the only part which is eaten.

COMMENTS: The leek is known throughout Europe and temperate Asia, common in northern China but less in the southern provinces. It has a mild, sweet flavor and a characteristically slippery texture.

   The Chinese consider the leek to have a warm, pungent energy that can warm and stimulate digestion, and that can particularly 'bring out the fragrance of meat', as one Cantonese has expressed it. In addition, raw leeks have a reputation for being able to cleanse the intestines of infections (e.g. dysentery, parasites), much the same as garlic, according to natives of Shantung. To cleanse the breath they recommend eating black dates (*naam jo*) or dried persimmons (*chee bang* 柿餅).

PREPARATION: Peel off and discard outer dirty, dried, or disfigured leaves; chop off tough upper greens. This leaves the pristine white heart of the vegetable to be chopped as desired. Rinse well or soak to remove any clinging grit. For Chinese uses, quarter lengthwise and chop in 2-inch lengths.

COOKING:

Western The French traditionally sauté leeks in butter as a side dish; the Welsh combine them with potatoes to make soup. In addition, they can be stuffed, baked, braised, or blanched and served with vinaigrette.

Chinese In Peking restaurants, strips of raw leek are served together with cucumber and rolled together with slices of duck in Peking pancakes. Shantung people eat them raw; Cantonese people stir-fry or braise them—commonly with beef. In general, leeks can be treated like onions or garlic chives (*gau choi* and *gau wong*) and cooked with a range of meats and other vegetables. In any case, don't let them brown in the cooking lest they become bitter, and don't let them cook too long lest they become slimy.

WATER SPINACH   *Ong choi* 蕹菜

APPEARANCE: Identify water spinach by its jointed hollow stems and arrowhead-shaped leaves. There are two varieties that differ slightly in color, leaf shape, and form. The variety illustrated here is *soi ong choi*, and has relatively thick stems, a light green color, and larger leaves. The other variety, *hon ong choi*, has more slender stems, darker color, and narrower leaves.

QUALITY: Within either variety the shorter the stalks and the larger the leaves at the tip, the more tender.

COMMENTS: Calling this 'spinach' is misleading because this is not even in the same botanical family as true spinach. Gastronomically speaking, it is appropriate because both are simple, popular, common, prosaic 'greens'. Water spinach is grown and eaten throughout Southeast Asia. It has a mild flavor and smooth texture; its most outstanding and potentially endearing characteristic is the contrast in texture between stem (crunchy) and leaves (limp) when cooked.

Water spinach appears in Hong Kong markets from mid-spring to mid-autumn. Popular, abundant, and inexpensive, it is nevertheless considered strictly summer food. Chinese nutritionists describe it as 'cooling' and diuretic. Housewives simply know it tastes best cooked with something of intense and 'warming'—i.e. spicy, pungent, or fermented—flavor.

LEAFY VEGETABLES

48

In serving water spinach two consequences of its high water content should be considered. First, plan to use what you buy within a few days because the leaves quickly yellow and succumb to soggy rot. Wrapping the veg in a cotton towel before enclosing in a plastic bag can slow but not prevent this decay. Second, as it cooks, it shrinks to a mere and literal shadow of its fresh self, so wash up heaps in order to have more than a spoonful to serve.

PREPARATION: Wash carefully as this grows in marshy situations where it provides refuge for a host of microbes, snails, and other creatures. Discard lowest 1–2 inches of stems, which are more than likely too tough to eat; edible stem will snap easily between your fingers. Continue to snap (rather than chop) the stalks into bite-size bits. Traditional cooks crush the thick stems of *soi ong choi* as they do this in order to facilitate cooking.

COOKING:

Western Treat as you would ordinary spinach: sauté with butter and garlic, or with bacon, and toss with a little vinegar and sugar. A piquant condiment such as mustard or Worcestershire sauce complements it well.

Chinese Although other Asians serve water spinach in a variety of ways—in soup, batter-fried, raw, etc.—the Cantonese exclusively stir-fry it, with a generous amount of garlic (or garlic shallots) and either white fermented bean curd or fermented shrimp sauce; chilli is common but optional.

STIR-FRIED WATER SPINACH
1 clove garlic, crushed
1/2 catty water spinach
Seasoning: Use any ONE of the following. Quantities are suggestions only. Alter according to personal taste, after experimentation:
> 1/2 cube white fermented bean curd (*fu yu* 腐乳)
> OR 1 tsp dried shrimp paste (*ha go* 蝦羔)
> OR 1 tbsp shrimp sauce (*ha jeung* 蝦醬)

With a rather generous amount of hot oil in wok, fry garlic until fragrant; discard. Add vegetable (the roar of moisture meeting hot oil should be deafening). Toss until wilted. Add chosen seasoning plus a pinch of sugar (and chilli); toss to combine, then cover and cook until done.

For faster and more even distribution, you may mix the seasoning to a thick sauce with water before adding. The entire cooking operation should take no more than 3–4 minutes over fierce heat. No extra salt should be necessary as all of the suggested seasonings are themselves quite salty.

CHINESE SPINACH *Een choi* 莧菜

APPEARANCE: As illustrated, this vegetable is typically sold as entire plants—shoot plus root. The cultivated varieties are generally large, 6–10 inches in length, with oval leaves that may be green or green with dark red centres.

In addition, in Hong Kong, a small 4–5-inch version of this vegetable sometimes reaches outlying markets. It too is sold as entire plants; leaves are oval but much smaller, and the plant may be dominated by granular flower-and-seed stalks. This is a wild species, related to the cultivated one. Preparation and cooking are the same; flavor is generally stronger; vitamins and minerals are probably more; shelf life is definitely shorter.

QUALITY: Select plants with many and large leaves. The red-leaved variety is considered by some to be more choice, but it tastes and generally costs the same.

COMMENTS: This is Amaranth, a genus of plants that has been cultivated for centuries, in Asia for its leaves and in Latin America for its seed, eaten as a grain. The greens have a distinct and pleasant flavor, and a coarse but tender texture, which to many is preferable to that of true spinach.

For the Chinese, this is grown and consumed exclusively during the summer. Chinese nutritionists reckon it can reduce internal heat and remove dampness—two intractable problems during hot sticky weather. Chemical analysis reveals it is exceptionally high in protein, rivalling most podded beans and root crops (unusual for a leaf), and also has noteworthy amounts of vitamin A, calcium, and iron.

Because *een choi* is sold as whole plants, it keeps better than most leafy vegetables. Wrap the plants in a damp towel, encase in a plastic bag, and store in the fridge; with luck, they will keep for a week.

PREPARATION: Break off the roots; soak the shoots in water and go over them carefully to remove grit, especially lodged at the leaf bases.

COOKING:

Western Cook as you would—or in any recipe as a substitute for—spinach. Most simply boil or steam it briefly, drain, and season. More elaborately, sauté with bacon; bake *au gratin* with cheese or seafood; mince as a filling for quiche or pastries; purée for soup. A little garlic or onion enhances flavor greatly.

Chinese Cantonese cooks invariably prepare and serve this green simply: either stir-fried, or in soup. In both cases garlic is the *sine qua non* of success. For stir-frying, mince a generous amount of garlic or, preferably, garlic shallots (*suen jee*, p 23); toss this into the hot oil before the vegetable. Season with salt or white fermented bean curd cheese, *fu yu* (in the latter case, add also a pinch of sugar).

For soup, simply toss a handful of leaves into broth. The Cantonese keep it simple, using lean pork for flavor, but other meats, fish, or vegetables can serve the purpose equally well.

EGG AND SPINACH HOTPOT
Chinese spinach
1 fresh chicken egg
1 salted duck egg (*haam daan* 鹹蛋)
1 clove garlic

Crush the clove of garlic; fry it in a small amount of oil in a saucepan. Add the vegetable; stir until just wilted. Add the chicken stock or water—to about half the depth of the vegetable if you want a casserole, or to float the vegetable if you want a soup. Bring to a boil and simmer until vegetable is 80 per cent cooked, only 2–3 minutes. Meanwhile, clean the duck egg by washing or scraping off the black powder. Break it into a bowl; remove the yolk (which should be rather firm, as though cooked already), chop into small pieces, and add to the soup. Add the chicken egg to the salted egg white, beat to mix, then add this too into the soup. Serve.

CHINESE BOX THORN   *Gau gei choi* 枸杞菜

APPEARANCE: Identify this vegetable by its stiff, straight, stout, unbranched stems. Oval leaves closely cover the branches, giving them the appearance of slim feather dusters. They typically measure 15–20 inches in length—and sometimes bear thorns hidden among the foliage.

QUALITY: The main criterion is a bushy green look of healthy vigor.

COMMENTS: Also known as matrimony vine, this plant belongs to a family (the *Solanaceae*) of considerable diversity and economic importance, including, for example, the potato, tomato, petunia, and tobacco. Interestingly, just as the potato and tomato were first grown for ornamentation, not eating, so Chinese box thorn is grown as a decorative shrub in American and European gardens and as a food plant only in Asia.

In terms of flavor, texture, and even nutrition, this is the closest thing to true spinach Asia has to offer. It has a mild flavor, smooth texture, and rich chemistry: higher in protein than other common leafy greens, and loaded with calcium and iron. (Unlike spinach, however, it is unusually rich in natural sodium, and cannot be eaten raw).

According to the Chinese, this vegetable—as well as the fruits of the same shrub (available dried in herb shops under the name *gau gei jee*)—are valuable liver tonics. Drinking soup made from this vegetable is particularly and widely reputed to sharpen eyesight. Relatively powerful both in flavor and effect, box thorn soup is served on an occasional rather than daily basis.

PREPARATION: First check for thorns; then defoliate the stems by grasping the tip with one hand and running your hand down its length—carefully if thorns were detected. Save the leaves, discard the stems.

COOKING:

Western Make soup in the Asian tradition. You may either wilt the leaves in oil lightly, then add stock; or add leaves to simmering stock. The latter creates a slightly more bitter brew. Use a rather richly flavored broth, or mix with other greens to modulate the flavor. A dash of pungency—ginger or pepper—and a pinch of sugar accents it nicely.

Chinese The single most popular and common way in which Hong Kong Cantonese cook and serve this vegetable is in soup made with pork liver, as described below. The ginger and pepper presumably function both to kill any off-flavors or odors from the liver, and to stimulate cleansing circulation through the liver. More importantly, they say, it just tastes better that way.

Box Thorn Soup
1/2 cup fresh pork liver
Ginger juice
4 cups box thorn leaves
White pepper
5–6 cups water

Slice the liver thinly and marinate with sugar, salt, cornstarch, and fresh ginger juice. Heat a small amount of oil in a saucepan. Add the leaves and stir until wilted. Add water; bring to the boil and simmer about 5 minutes. Add liver, and continue to simmer 2–3 minutes until liver is just cooked. Season with salt and a liberal dash of pepper. Serve.

CEYLON SPINACH   *Saan choi* 潺菜

APPEARANCE: A combination of rather subtle characteristics distinguish this vegetable from the green leafy cabbages. Note that, in this vegetable, both stems and leaves have the same bright green color; that the leaves themselves are broad in shape and rather rubbery in texture; and that no flowers are present. Finally, note the peculiar but characteristic wide U-shape with which the leaf stalks join the stem.

QUALITY: Select young tender plants, characterized by bright color, lack of blemishes, and large leaves.

COMMENTS: The most accurate translation of the Chinese name for this vegetable, *saan*, is mucilaginous, and this adjective quite accurately describes its texture. The taste is mild and inoffensive, but the feeling of it in the mouth is not universally popular.
A second translation of the word *saan* is slippery—which is also appropriate, since it is reputed to be a mild laxative.

PREPARATION: Wash the leaves well; break stems between leaves into bite-size chunks for cooking.

COOKING: Most Asians, including the Cantonese, appear to use *saan choi* primarily in soup. Other ethnic groups might consider it a substitute for okra, for example in Indian curries or in American Cajun dishes.

SLIPPERY SOUP
Heat a small amount of oil in a saucepan. Add a slice of fresh ginger; when fragrant, add water or chicken stock and bring to the boil. Add *saan choi*, using about 1 cup of vegetable per 1–2 cups of liquid; fresh bean curd may also be added. Simmer 5–10 minutes, season with salt and white pepper, and serve.

Instead of salt, you may add a salted duck egg (*haam daan*)—one egg per 3–4 cups of soup—to impart flavor, variety, and protein to the final brew.

53

PEA SHOOTS *Dau miu* 豆苗

APPEARANCE: In the market this vegetable appears in rather forlorn heaps. Each shoot comprises a short stem bearing pairs of small, limp oval leaflets, curling tendrils and an occasional white flower. (N.B. Alfalfa shoots, *muk sook,* are also sold in some Shanghai stores; these are of the same size, shape, and color but have leaves of three leaflets.)

QUALITY: Buy the smallest, most tender ones you can find. These may also be the most wilted ones around, but they will be the most tender. As warm weather approaches, the stems thicken and the shoots become tough: time to serve another vegetable.

COMMENTS: Pleasant taste, tender texture, bright color, limited season, and short shelf life are the qualities that give pea shoots their gastronomic status. Botanically, these shoots are the growing tips of ordinary green pea plants. Horticulturally, the plants are grown as creepers rather than upright vines, and are prevented from flowering or fruiting. Thus, lacking adult fibre, the shoots wilt as soon as they are picked. For best results, store them loosely tossed in a plastic box, and use them within 2–3 days of purchase (or plucking).

Neither Western nor Chinese nutritionists seem to have definitive comments on this vegetable. Evidence so far suggests that the wallet is the only organ that suffers when this vegetable is consumed. Fortunately ill effects are soon forgotten.

PREPARATION: Wash and drain.

COOKING:

Western Steam or sauté in butter, and season with salt and pepper. Substitute for spinach in Florentine dishes, particularly those with seafood. Bake in white sauce *au gratin*, or serve with a cream, cheese, or mustard sauce.

Chinese Among Hong Kong Cantonese, *dau miu* is strictly winter food. And until affluence, horticultural wizardry, and efficient marketing made them affordable, they were served only on special occasions. In homes they may be parboiled in broth flavored with lean pork and liver, or simply stir-fried with fresh ginger. Restaurants are more apt to serve them with other expensive ingredients such as snake or crab meat, as described below.

DAU MIU WITH SEAFOOD SAUCE
3–4 cups pea shoots
1 cup cooked crab, lobster, shrimp (or other white-fleshed fish)
1 egg white, lightly beaten
1 cup light stock (or water plus chicken bouillon cube)
(White wine or cooking sherry)
(Sesame oil)

With a minimum of oil, stir-fry pea shoots and mound on serving dish. In wok or sauce-pan, combine stock with 1 tablespoon cornstarch; heat, stirring constantly. As sauce thickens, add shreds of seafood and season with (a dash of sesame oil, a dash of wine) salt and white pepper. Simmer gently and briefly. When mixture seems thoroughly cooked, add egg white while stirring vigorously to break the white into shreds as it coagulates. Adjust seasoning, pour sauce over shoots, and serve.

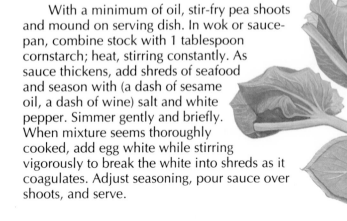

LETTUCE   *Saang choi* 生菜

APPEARANCE: Leaf lettuce, as illustrated, comes in many varieties. Leaves vary in shape from broad to narrow, with edges jagged or smooth. Note, however, that all lack distinct leaf stalks (midribs, yes; leaf stalks or petioles, no) and have a rather thin texture. These characteristics together with overall shape distinguish lettuce from other greens, particularly mustard cabbages.

QUALITY: Hot weather and/or old age cause lettuce plants to produce flowers, bitter chemicals, and tough leaves. Logically, then, bunches with short stems, large leaves, and no evidence of flower stalks are the sweetest and most tender.

COMMENTS: Botanically, the genus of lettuce is *Lactuca*, a name that derives from the Latin name for milk, *lac*, and which refers to the white sap characteristic of all its species. *L. sativa*, the widely cultivated salad crop of today, probably originated in the Middle East. It may have been grown for its seeds, was definitely used for its narcotic sap, and first appeared on the dinner table in Persia around 550 BC. Some thousand years later it reached China.

Today, although more than a hundred varieties of lettuce exist, the Chinese stick to one or two. They reckon this is a cooling, faintly bitter vegetable that can relieve stomach heat but 'attack' the liver if eaten in excess. Hence, it is appropriate for serving in hot weather or with heating foods (e.g. hamburgers, oyster sauce), and cooked in or dressed with oil.

The Chinese have another reason to serve lettuce, above and beyond its nutritional effects. The Chinese name for lettuce, pronounced *saang choi* in Cantonese, is a homonym: the word *choi* can mean either vegetable or money depending on the tone with which you say it, while *saang* can mean either fresh or first. Thus, as quite an auspicious vegetable, lettuce is served to the family on birthdays, New Year's Day, graduation days and other festive occasions, and is offered to the obstreperous lion in traditional Lion Dances.

PREPARATION: Separate leaves; wash thoroughly, particularly at the leaf bases.

COOKING: Head and leaf lettuce are interchangeable, raw or cooked, although results vary according to their differences in taste and texture. Whenever cooking lettuce of any sort, (1) do it quickly, over high heat, in order to serve it green, sweet, and crunchy; and (2) anticipate great shrinkage.

Western Raw, a mixed salad of leaf and head lettuces combines the best of taste and texture of both. Cooked, lettuce can substitute for grape leaves in making Greek *dolma* or for cabbage leaves in making braised stuffed rolls.

Chinese Cantonese ways with lettuce can be reduced to three categories: as envelopes for *saang choi bau* described below; as a side dish or member thereof; as an ingredient in soup or congee.

As a vegetable, lettuce may be parboiled or stir-fried; with only ginger and garlic; with fresh mushrooms; with dried winter mushrooms; with chicken, beef, pork, liver, or other viscera. It may garnish a platter or support a richly flavored sauce of braised scallops, of deep-fried pigeon eggs, of oysters (i.e. oyster sauce), or of fresh shrimp and spring onions. Lettuce, fish, and bean curd are a common combination of complementary tastes and textures that are eaten as soup, congee (see below), stew, and stir-fry dishes.

For soup, use virtually any combination of the ingredients mentioned above to flavor the broth, then add the lettuce last in order to cook it only briefly before serving.

FRESH FISH CONGEE

Rice: preferably short grain and white; neither long-grain nor brown disintegrates properly. Use approximately 1/4 cup per serving.

(1–2 dried scallops, *gong yu chu* 江瑤柱 , soaked)

(Chicken bones or meat)

In quantities to taste: Fish fillet of mild flavor and best quality, cut in small pieces
Lettuce, thinly shredded
Ginger, finely shredded
Spring onions, minced

To make congee, put rice in large pot with approximately 8–10 times as much water as rice. Add scallops and chicken if desired. Bring to boil and simmer rather vigorously, partially covered, 1–2 hours until porridge is thick and individual rice grains have disintegrated. During cooking, if steam pressure builds up inside, foam will bubble out the top. Chinese soup pots have a hole in the lid to provide the ventilation that prevents this; with a rice cooker or saucepan, prop the lid open by sandwiching a chopstick between rim and lid to one side of pot. Alternatively, modern Cantonese cooks recommend making congee in a crockpot. This method produces a creamier congee, but taste suffers, perhaps from lack of exercise in the simmering.

When the congee has reached the desired, creamy consistency of oat porridge or pea soup, it is ready. Add fish; when it returns to the boil, add lettuce. Season with salt, white pepper, and a little cooked oil. As soon as fish and lettuce are cooked, serve. At the table provide ginger, spring onions, and light soy sauce for each diner to season his portion to taste.

CORN CONGEE

One of the most popular dishes in Cantonese vegetarian restaurants is this chowder-like gruel. Prepare plain congee as above. Toward the end of the cooking, add corn of some sort—either cut from a cob, canned, creamed, or frozen. At the last moment, add the lettuce, some frozen peas for color, and a few slices of Chinese doughnuts (*yau ja gwai*) or other crisp (and ideally greasy) condiment for textural interest.

CREATIVE CONGEE

Although the Cantonese usually combine lettuce only with fish in congee, non-Cantonese are free to combine it with anything. There's even the seasonal Turkey Congee, a traditional delicacy found only in certain American homes toward the end of November, and again in December.

BIRTHDAY LETTUCE

Lettuce, chopped or torn into pieces
Winter mushrooms, soaked
Bean curd, each large square quartered
Ginger
Oyster sauce

In a minimum of very hot oil, stir-fry lettuce and remove. Heat more oil, and brown bean curd on all sides. Add mushrooms, shreds or thin, crushed slices of ginger, any liquid that has accumulated under the lettuce, mushroom-soaking liquid, and a generous splash of oyster sauce. Cover; braise briefly. Uncover; thicken sauce with a cornstarch paste, season with soy sauce, drizzle with a dash of sesame oil, scoop onto lettuce, and serve.

MEAL IN A LEAF

The idea is to spread a minced filling with sauce on a raw lettuce leaf, roll, and eat. The filling is classically minced pigeon meat and bamboo shoots, seasoned with garlic, ginger, wine and soy sauce to give it red color. Adding minced pork and mushrooms is also known, as is the fact that virtually any minced pork, beef, chicken, fish or shellfish filling with or without chopped jicama, winter mushrooms, onions, etc will do. For a strictly vegetarian filling, nuts (e.g. peanuts, cashews, sunflower seeds, walnuts), carrots, peas, and celery go well together.

In any recipe, remember to use richly flavored ingredients, to chop them finely, and either to cook the sauce well into the ingredients or thicken it with starch, in order to make it manageable for rolling and eating.

WHITE WORMWOOD *Jun jiu choi* 珍珠菜

APPEARANCE: Distinguish this vegetable by the 8–10-inch long reddish-purple leaf stalks and sparse, triple-leafletted leaf blades. There is no stem: these are individual leaves.

QUALITY: Select well-formed leaves that appear freshly picked. The more leaf blade per stalk the better.

COMMENTS: These leaves have a strong, rather resinous or 'floral' taste slightly similar to chrysanthemum leaves. In fact, they come from plants of the same botanical family as chrysanthemum and lettuce, and of the same genus as true wormwood or absinthe.

The resinous taste is bitter, which suggests a metabolic effect of 'cooling' the body and cleansing the blood, and which rather restricts the ways it is served. In fact, *jun jiu choi* is generally served in only two ways: either deep-fried, when the strong taste of the oil mitigates the taste of the vegetable; or boiled in a tonic soup.

PREPARATION: Wash and chop, discarding toughest lower portions of leaf stalks.

COOKING: Deep-fried wormwood is a specialty of Chiu Chow (Swatow) cuisine in which it is served generously bordering platters of Chiu Chow chicken, another specialty. Other Cantonese use this vegetable simply to make soup, by tossing the leaves into broth flavored with slices of lean pork. Two or three leaf stalks per bowl of broth are sufficient. Simmer briefly to cook leaves thoroughly, season with salt, and serve.

GARLAND CHRYSANTHEMUM   *Tong ho* 茼蒿

APPEARANCE: A casual glance might cause one to mistake chrysanthemum for Chinese cabbage or leaf lettuce. Note, however, that chrysanthemum leaves are bluntly lobed, uniformly green, and rather rough (not shiny smooth). It is usually sold as a small plant, with root still attached, which is never true of cabbage.

QUALITY: Select plants with unblemished crisp leaves, preferably without signs of flowering.

COMMENTS: Technically, according to some experts, the multitudes of cultivated chrysanthemums can be reduced to only two species: one provides flowers (in uncountable varieties created by horticultural selection and breeding), while the other provides vegetables. Within the edible species three varieties exist: one that the Japanese grow for leaves; one that the Chinese grow for leaves; and one that the Chinese grow for flowers, used fresh to garnish snake dishes or dried in tea and herbal medicines.

Chrysanthemum leaves have an unmistakable and somewhat resinous flavor, which is perhaps best enjoyed in small quantities amidst other foods. The Cantonese respect it for its ability to warm and 'harmonize' the stomach, which in turn warms the entire body. Hence, it is served primarily in the winter, with hotpots and snake dishes, as a means of stimulating the digestion of these rich dishes.

PREPARATION: Separate leaves from central stalk, which is generally discarded. Wash well.

COOKING: Hunan Chinese sometimes stir-fry *tong ho* as a vegetable on its own; Cantonese generally use it only in hotpots or soup. For a quick version of the latter, simply flavor boiling water with shreds of lean pork or chicken (or use stock, or some sort of bouillon cube), add the chrysanthemum—either alone or with other suitably mild-flavored vegetables such as bean curd, lettuce, or fresh mushrooms—season with light soy sauce, and serve.

Alternatively, you may let your guests cook their own meal, as described below. This soup-fondue is a traditional Cantonese meal enjoyed in restaurants and homes alike, exclusively in the winter when the steaming pot both cooks the food and warms the diners.

Cantonese Hotpot (Da Been Lo)

Ingredients:
A selection of fresh vegetables, prepared in bite-size pieces, such as:
    Bean curd
    Lettuce
    Peking cabbage
    Mung bean sprouts
    Chrysanthemum leaves
A selection of very fresh meat, sliced as thinly as possible, such as:
    Beef
    Pork
    Chicken
    Liver
    Squid or cuttlefish
Mung bean vermicelli, soaked
Winter mushrooms, soaked
Noodles

Condiments: Small dishes of sauces for dipping, such as light soy sauce, chilli sauce, mustard, sesame oil, beaten raw egg.

Equipment:
1 pot of boiling water with heat source strong enough to keep the water simmering throughout the cooking, e.g. a rice cooker, charcoal hibachi, or portable gas burner.
Cooking implements, one per diner, e.g. fondue forks, skewers, small wire baskets with long handles (sold in Chinese stores expressly for this purpose), or wooden chopsticks.

Procedure: Place the pot in the center of the table; add the mushrooms, cover, and bring to a boil. Add some of each of the vegetables and vermicelli at this point, and periodically throughout the meal. Cooking the meat proceeds as with a French fondue; that is, each person skewers a morsel and dips it: raw, into the broth; when cooked, into a sauce; and when cool, into his mouth. In some households the cooked morsels are dipped into raw beaten egg, and then wrapped in a raw lettuce leaf. As vegetables are eaten, add more; the mushrooms are generally left in, flavoring the broth until the end.

When that time comes, add the noodles to the pot. These, together with an exquisitely flavored bowl of soup, end the meal in grand style.

LONG BEANS   *Dau gok* 豆角

APPEARANCE: 'Long' means 1–3 feet in length. They come in two colors: light green, known as *baak dau gok* (白豆角) or 'white long beans'; and dark green, known as *cheng dau gok* (青豆角) or 'green long beans'. Because they are small and round in cross section and so long, they actually look more like string than the short beans that Americans have named 'string beans' because of the tough fibre running the length of some of them. (N.B. The Cantonese call this latter stringy bean *yook dau.*)

QUALITY: The darker ones are considered superior, but let frank evaluation of characteristics (see below), personal preference, and intended use guide purchase. In both cases, as with string beans, the smaller the swellings (i.e. beans growing inside) and the firmer the pod wall, the crunchier the texture and the sweeter the flavor.

COMMENTS: Botanically, these beans differ in genus and species from string beans, and in fact they are the pod in which cowpeas or black-eyed peas grow. They have been cultivated in China since before recorded time. Patient, northern Chinese grow them to maturity for dry peas, while the southerners prefer to cook the immature pods.

Long beans taste more or less like string beans. The big difference is texture. The dark green ones have a thin tight pod wall, and remain crunchy when cooked (or downright tough if undercooked). The lighter green ones have a thicker wall, which is more succulent—more like string beans—when young, but flabby and fibrous when old.

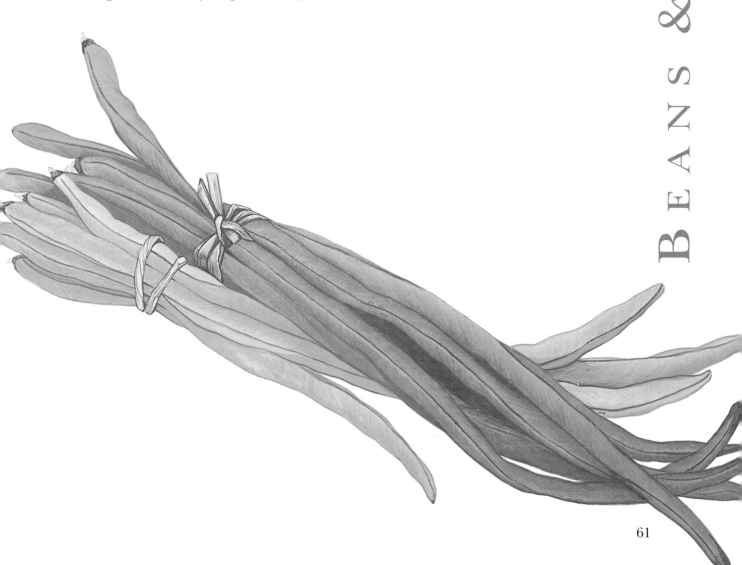

According to the Chinese, podded beans—both string and long types—have a neutral energy and a fundamentally sweet flavor, which is believed to tonify both stomach and kidneys. Hence, podded beans are considered good summer fare, and suitable complements for simple but rich companions such as eggs and shrimp.

PREPARATION: Wash; chop into 1-inch lengths for Chinese dishes, or as desired. Neither of these have the strings after which 'string beans' were named.

COOKING: Long beans may be unequivocally substituted for string beans, and vice-versa.

Western Nuts and seeds go well with beans. Stir-fry them together with a slice or two of carrot for color and soy sauce for flavor. Or purée them together with onions and carrot for pâté or patties. The more meaty light green beans are most like string beans, hence best for casseroles and such. The dark green ones are particularly good in cooked salads because they retain both color and texture after chilling. For this purpose you may parboil them whole, then tie into knots.

Chinese The Cantonese cook *dau gok* in one of three ways. First, and most commonly, they are stir-fried with egg. (Unlike preparing an omelette, stir-fry the beans first and add the beaten eggs last.) Second, they may be cooked in black bean sauce (see directions under 'garlic' p 20), generally but not necessarily with pork of some sort. Fresh straw mushrooms are a good addition to such a dish. Third, they are stir-fried at random with whatever else happens to be available, as in the following:

VEGETABLE MEDLEY
Peanuts
Long beans, chopped in 1-inch lengths
Celery, sliced thinly on the diagonal
Shrimp, cleaned and rubbed with a little (coarse) salt
Spring onions, chopped in 1-inch lengths

Heat oil; fry peanuts until almost golden; remove—they will cook completely as they drain. Remove excess oil from wok, leaving just enough for the vegetables. When oil is quite hot, stir-fry beans and celery, seasoning them with salt and a pinch of sugar; remove when just tender. Again heat oil; stir-fry shrimp quickly, return veg, peanuts, and spring onions. Toss, season, and serve.

PEAPODS: SNOW PEAS *Hoh laan dau* 荷蘭豆
HONEY OR SUGAR PEAS *Mut Dau* 蜜豆

APPEARANCE: Edible peapods measure 2–4 inches long and about 1 inch wide, with a stalk at one end and, often, the remains of the flower at the other. Snow peas, illustrated below, are flexible and flat, with bulges where the peas are growing. There are two types: robust and dainty. The robust peapods are about twice the size, both length and width, of the smaller ones.

Honey peas, in contrast, are rigid and oval in cross-section, more like shell peas or inflated balloons, with no external evidence of the peas inside.

QUALITY: Within any single variety, the smaller the pod and the smaller the peas inside the pod, the more tender and sweet the peapods. The smaller type of snow peas—which are more flexible in the fingers, and often still have bits of flowers at the tips—are generally younger, sweeter, and more tender. Honey peas are the most crisp, meaty, expensive, and rare.

COMMENTS: The belief that edible peapods are a quintessential and traditional Asian food seems to be an illusion. The Cantonese name *hoh laan*, a corruption of 'Holland', may more accurately indicate their origins, since the practice of eating the pods before the peas mature seems to have originated in Europe.

Like green beans, all peapods are edible, but the varieties grown for the purpose are more delectable because they lack a certain parchment-like layer that otherwise toughens the pod. In any case, peapods—particularly the honey peapods—are crisp in texture, verdant, and sweet.

Peapods are not a staple vegetable of Hong Kong Cantonese home cuisine. Perhaps they are too sweet; as a flavor, sweetness pleases the stomach but excess can disrupt the appetite. Like dessert, then, peapods are eaten occasionally and especially on festive occasions. Just as their vivid color is most appreciated as an accent, so their flavor is perhaps most appetizing in combination with other ingredients.

PREPARATION: Strings running lengthwise along both edges of the pod must be removed. Accomplish this efficiently by snapping the stem end off, leaving one string attached, tearing that string off top to bottom, then grasping and tearing the other string off bottom to top.

COOKING: A little oil goes a long way with peapods because they absorb virtually none—all remains on the outside. Use a minimum when sautéing or stir-frying, or instead opt for parboiling. Like the singularity of their flavor and the impermeability of their surface, peapods do not actually blend with other foods, either in flavor or texture. Use them accordingly for accent and contrast.

Western Nibble raw. Parboil or steam, and serve salted, peppered, and buttered. Sauté lightly with a sprig of mint, thyme, or basil. As with long and string beans, nuts go well with peapods, in salads or stir-fry.

Chinese The Cantonese stir-fry all of the three forms of this vegetable alone (with crushed bits of ginger and garlic), or with something else, either other vegetables and/or shreds of pork, beef, chicken, or liver. In restaurants, honey peas are usually served stir- fried with fresh seafood such as scallops or prawns. At Chinese New Year, peapods are the last ingredient added to the traditional mixed vegetable casserole, *Lo Hon Jai.*

In choosing stir-fry companions for peapods, consider flavor and texture. Anything absorbent is good textural contrast, for example, carrots and mushrooms; while those things pungent—e.g. ginger, garlic, radish—can wake up the somnolent sweetness.

SOY BEANS (FRESH) *Mo dau* 毛豆

APPEARANCE: These are small bean pods, 2–3 inches long, less than an inch wide, pale green, hairy, and with distinct indentations where the beans inside lie.

QUALITY: Select pods with firm, sound beans inside. Smaller beans are sweeter and more tender, but take longer to shell. Don't worry too much about the state of the pod, which can turn yellow and develop black spots without damaging the beans inside—which is what you're after.

COMMENTS: Known and served primarily in the temperate regions of Asia where they grow, fresh soy beans are a sweet, tender, and nutritious treat.

As with other soy forms and products (e.g. soy bean sprouts, bean curd), these beans are slightly poisonous raw and slightly 'cooling' even when cooked. Hence, a bit of ginger will warm the stomach to its task of digestion, and a bit of sea vegetable or fish in the meal will counteract soy's tendency to depress thyroid gland function.

PREPARATION: For most purposes, shell them. For serving as snacks, leave whole.

COOKING:
Western Use these as you would baby lima beans, which they mightily resemble. Toss them in stir-fry dishes; combine in casseroles and soups; parboil for salads or marinated vegetable mixtures.

Asian In Japan and northern China, entire pods are parboiled and served as a snack, with soy sauce for dipping. (Happily, this transfers the tedium of shelling from cook to consumer.) Otherwise these beans appear in stir-fry dishes with meat or other soy-derived products, and particularly in Shanghai-style cold snacks, such as the one described below:

Snow Cabbage & Soy Beans
Approximately equal proportions of:
    Fresh soy beans
    Pressed bean curd
    Preserved snow cabbage (*suet lui hoeng* 雪裏紅)
    (Chilli)
    Sesame oil

Shell, then parboil the soy beans 5 minutes. Slice bean curd into thin strips. Chop the preserved cabbage coarsely. In hot oil (preferably at least part of which is sesame) in the wok, stir-fry bean curd and soy beans 2–3 minutes. Then add the preserved cabbage (and chilli). Continue to cook vigorously for several minutes until flavors seem to have blended, adding water in small quantities as required to facilitate the cooking. Dish. This can be served hot or, as is the usual custom, cold.

MUNG BEAN SPROUTS *Nga choi* 芽菜

APPEARANCE: Sprouts are readily recognized as tender, translucent shafts with a root at one end and a seed at the other. Hong Kong vendors sell three sorts: two with beans attached, and one without. Of the two with beans, the larger ones with oval yellow heads are soy bean sprouts (q.v.), while the smaller ones with round green heads are mung bean sprouts. The bean-less sprouts are mung bean sprouts with the bean removed (by hand) and are called silver sprouts or *ngun nga choi*.

QUALITY: Fresh bean sprouts are translucent white from head to tail, and form crisp-looking jumbled mounds. Young, tender sprouts are relatively short and fat, with no evidence of leaves emerging from between the bean halves.

COMMENTS: Sprouting changes any seed's flavor, texture, chemistry, and hence nutritional value, by transforming starches into vitamins, sugars, and tender young plant. From the Chinese point of view, sprouting transforms a condensed form (seed) into an expanded form (sprout), from dry to wet, from slowly to actively metabolizing. All of these latter characteristics are associated with cooling and cleansing effects on the body. This, coupled with the fact that the mung bean itself is considered to have cool, detoxifying properties, means that mung sprouts are downright cold in energy. Cooked alone, they cool: this is appropriate for counteracting conditions of heat in the body (inflammation, burns, food poisoning), but not if a body is already cool (e.g. winter weakness, anemia). Hence, to achieve balance in ordinary cooking, combine mung sprouts with warming ingredients or serve them with other, 'warmer' dishes.

Silver sprouts, like bread without the crust, are considered finer than whole sprouts. They cook slightly more evenly and quickly, and look more uniform when served. Thus restaurants always serve them; they are preferred for filling spring rolls (or 'egg rolls' as American Chinese restaurants call them); but ordinary housewives seldom consider them worth the extra price.

When storing sprouts, preserve their youthful nature by keeping them covered with water in a covered container in the fridge. Ordinary sprouts will keep several days in this way. Silver sprouts, on the other hand, can hardly be stored at all because trimming initiates irreversible and rapid deterioration of flavor and texture.

PREPARATION: If time allows, remove unsightly tails; if ceremony dictates, remove heads too. Rinse and drain. Do not bother purposefully to remove the green seed coats of the beans but if they happen to float away as you wash them, be happy.

COOKING: In preparing mung bean sprouts remember that they are mostly water. Thus, their flavor is mild, they shrink as they cook, and liquid released during cooking must be dealt with. They do not absorb flavors, so the selection of what you cook them with and/or the creation of sauce is critical to success.

Western Mung sprouts can be eaten raw tossed in salads. Or they may be blanched, sautéed, and/or marinated. For seasoning, choose warming herbs such as would be appropriate for other bean dishes, e.g. thyme, savory, cumin, chilli.

Chinese Budding Western chefs typically begin their Chinese culinary careers cooking mung bean sprouts, little realizing that this is one of the most difficult vegetables to cook well. To produce a crisp and tasty bean sprout dish requires: first, crisp, fresh raw materials; second, a burner capable of intense heat; and third, skill in food combining and seasoning. The hot burner will cook the sprouts quickly and evaporate water before it can accumulate, stew the vegetable, and dilute the sauce.

As for food combining, choose 'warming', solid, and/or dry companions: virtually any meat, cut in thin slivers, will do (the Shanghainese particularly like eel with sprouts; the Cantonese like roasted pork, *cha siu*, with theirs); carrots are excellent, also cut in slivers; or spring onions; or mushrooms, which absorb flavors the way a sprout never can.

As versatile as they are insipid, bean sprouts can be stir-fried alone, with meat, poultry, fish, seafood, or simply with other vegetables. One of the most common Cantonese versions is a mixture of sprouts, shredded pork, mushrooms, and spring onions, which comes served atop a bed of deep-fried mung bean vermicelli. Sprouts are also omelette material (see below) and a wonderful addition to fried noodles, where the mouth discerns them but not the eye.

CHINESE OMELETTE
1 tbsp ham OR carrot, cut in slivers
(Winter mushrooms, soaked, cut in slivers)
(Spring onions, cut in 1-inch lengths)
(Ginger, shredded)
2–3 cups mung bean sprouts
2 eggs, lightly beaten and seasoned with salt and pepper

In hot oil in wok, over high heat, fry ham (or carrot, and any other ingredients desired) lightly. When done, add sprouts (ginger, spring onions), and toss. When sprouts are shiny, wilting, and almost cooked, pour eggs over and stir. For a moist result, at this point, simply extinguish heat, cover, and wait; the heat of the pan and the vegetables should set the egg within minutes. For a drier product, continue to cook over heat.

Prepared properly, this dish is mainly crisp sprouts, lightly bound together by a soft, delicately ham-flavored egg custard.

FRIED NOODLES WITH SPROUTS
Noodles: either white rice noodles (*hoh fun* 河粉) OR wheat noodles
Mung bean sprouts
Spring onions or blanched garlic chives (*gau wong* 韭黃)
Pork or beef, thinly sliced and marinated

Cook and drain noodles. With hot oil in wok, cook meat until almost done; remove. In more oil, add cooked noodles, toss, then sprouts and spring onions; season with soy sauce. Continue to stir and toss until flavors have blended and noodles are warmed through.

For a popular lunch dish, use wide *hoh fun*; use beef; and season with *sadeh* sauce (沙爹醬).

66

SOY BEAN SPROUTS *Dai dau nga choi* 大豆芽菜

APPEARANCE: *Nga choi* are bean sprouts; *dai* means big; *dau* are beans. Thus, not coincidentally, shoppers identify these sprouts by the big bean at one end. They may be further distinguished from mung bean sprouts by their general robustness (4–5 inches long) and, in Hong Kong, by an organized method of display. Where mung sprouts are invariably jumbled in a heap, soy sprouts are often neatly tied in bunches or arranged in a circle, heads to the outside and root-tails to the inside.

QUALITY: The beans should be yellow with no tint of green or hint of emerging leaves. The shoot should be clear white from head to tip.

COMMENTS: Soy bean sprouts are one of the most nutritious and economical foods available. Unlike other vegetables, soy beans have high levels of protein and oil, which make them comparable in food value to meat and eggs, and which give them a rich, nutty taste. The process of sprouting converts much of their already minimal starch into vitamins (particularly vitamin C), enzymes, and tender, sweet new plant.

Nevertheless, in the Chinese understanding, although soy beans are nutritious, they share qualities with other beans that must be considered in cooking and consuming them. The first of these the Cantonese describe as *hon*, a sort of debilitating coldness that disrupts the function of the stomach. The antidote is ginger. So dishes with soy beans, or soy sprouts (or even bean curd) typically require a slice, if not a hunk, of ginger to generate digestive heat. The second is a calming effect, which perhaps correlates with experimental reports that soy beans suppress the functioning of the thyroid gland. The antidote in this case is seaweed, or fish, or other iodine-rich food.

When storing sprouts, they will keep longer and remain whiter if stored covered with water in a covered container in the fridge.

PREPARATION: Trim off the lower root portions. This is most efficiently done *en masse* rather than sprout by sprout. Align the sprouts in a bunch on a chopping board and 'cut off their tails with a butcher's knife', as the rhyme goes. Then rinse and drain.

COOKING: In preparing soy sprouts, remember that these are not simply big mung sprouts. Think of them as a form of soy bean rather than as a form of sprout—for three reasons. First, soy sprouts (like all soy beans) are slightly poisonous raw, and hence must be cooked before consumption. Second, the bean is the best part—as rich and crunchy as a peanut. Third, the sprout itself, even the most eligible, tends to be tough and stringy rather than crisp and tender after cooking.

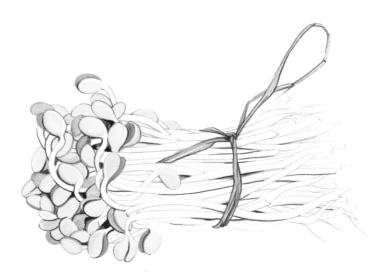

The best method for pre-cooking soy sprouts is by parching in a hot, dry wok or frying pan. In this way the sprouts reach a higher temperature than they would by boiling, and the flavor benefits immensely. Simply put the trimmed sprouts in the hot, dry pan; stir and toss, uncovered, until the sprouts have wilted and they smell cooked, 2–3 minutes.

Western After thorough parching, marinate in an oil and vinegar dressing. Sauté. Or, mince and combine with other minced vegetables (or meat) to make a loaf, patties, stuffing for green peppers or cabbage leaves, or casseroles. Minced finely, the shoots blend into such mixtures undetectably, whereas chopped coarsely, the beans add richness and crunch.

Chinese Three styles of preparation of this vegetable seem standard among the Cantonese: simply stir–fried with ginger (and pork, optional); boiled with pork bones to make a traditional 'poor man's' soup stock; and minced with pork in a meat patty.

PORK & SOY SPROUT SOUP
Pork bones or meat
Soy bean sprouts
1–2 slices of fresh ginger, crushed

Parch soy sprouts as described above. Then combine all ingredients and boil until broth is well-flavored—several hours for bones, less for meat. Season with salt or soy sauce.

N.B. Interestingly enough, even after long boiling, the beans remain whole, crunchy, and eminently edible.

PORK & SOY SPROUT MINCE
1/2 lb lean pork, minced, seasoned
1/2–1 lb soy bean sprouts, parched and minced
(2–3 winter mushrooms, soaked, chopped)
(2 tsp dried shrimp, soaked, chopped)
1 slice of fresh ginger, crushed

In hot oil, fry shrimp, then add mushrooms, then sprouts and the ginger. Toss and continue cooking over medium heat 3–4 minutes until done; remove. Reheat oil, fry meat, return vegetables, stir and toss. Adjust seasoning with soy sauce and, when flavors are thoroughly blended, dish and serve.

SOY SPROUT CASSEROLE
Soy bean sprouts
Carrot
Kelp
(Winter mushrooms, soaked, chopped)
Ginger

Parch soy sprouts; mince shoots but leave heads whole. Chop an approximately equal volume of carrot in approximately equivalent sized pieces. Soak a small piece of kelp, then chop. In a casserole, sauté mushrooms, if desired; then add soy sprouts, carrot, kelp, and a slice of crushed ginger. Season with soy, add water to cover about half, cover the pot, and simmer quietly 30–40 minutes.

BEAN CURD *Dau fu* 豆腐

Like other vegetables, bean curd has evolved into varieties, of which three will be described on the following pages.

Fresh bean curd—alias *dofu* in Mandarin Chinese or *tofu* in Japanese—is produced from the water extract of yellow soy beans. The beans are first soaked, then pulverized in water. Solids are filtered out and the remaining liquid suspension is cooked briefly to detoxify soy beans' harmful components. Finally a coagulating agent is added that curdles the suspension—i.e. creates a solid from a liquid—by changing the structure of the proteins. The traditional coagulating agent was a byproduct of producing sea salt in Japan (*nigari*); in China they used calcium carbonate. Fresh curd is sold as is, or processed further by pressing, drying, frying, or fermenting.

Nutritionally, bean curd has the water-soluble vitamins, minerals, and proteins of soy beans without the starch. This sounds good but can build strong bodies only when two factors are taken into consideration in preparing it. First, its actual effect on metabolism, in the Chinese estimation, is calming rather than stimulating. Doctors say it cools and detoxifies; the man on the street will tell you it is *hon*, a term used to describe food which drives dry cold into the body. Ginger is the common and recommended antidote, added to bean curd dishes for flavor as well as to warm and stimulate digestion. (Iodine, in the form of seaweed or fish, is also a good adjunct to bean curd because it can stimulate the thyroid, which soy beans seem to depress. See comments for soy bean sprouts p 67.)

The second factor that threatens bean curd's nutritional value in practice is its bland flavor and insubstantial texture. Some people—including some Chinese—just can't stand it. The antidote here is frying, which can change both texture and taste, making the soft hard (or at least crisp and porous), and enriching the insipid.

FRESH BEAN CURD   *Soi dau fu* 水豆腐

APPEARANCE: Fresh bean curd is white, shiny, and smooth, with the consistency of stiff jello. In Asian markets it is sold from the wooden cloth-lined trays in which it is made. These trays are stacked during manufacturing; entire stacks are taken to market and gradually unstacked as the sheets of curd are cut into cubes and sold.

QUALITY: Fresh bean curd should be pure white and shiny, with a faint, clean fragrance of soy beans. Any sour odor indicates it has begun to go off; toward the end of a hot summer day entire bean curd stalls can smell faintly sour. If so, beware. Sourness is probably not poisonous but it does limit uses of the curd to fried and braised dishes, where rich flavors will overpower the weak.

COMMENTS: This is the most common, and perhaps the most versatile, type of bean curd. But it is versatile within the parameters of Chinese nutritional assessment (see comments for 'bean curd' p 69). Innately 'cool', bean curd needs a little fire and brimstone for balance. For example, the preserved mustard stem, *za choi*, is a perfect complement. This preserved vegetable is hard where bean curd is soft, crunchy where bean curd is smooth, and intensely salty-sour-pungent where bean curd is perfectly bland.

Storing bean curd can be a problem because, left unattended, it sours. There are two good ways to prevent this. The first is to parboil it. As soon as you return from market, put the curd in a saucepan, cover with water, bring to the boil, allow to simmer 2–3 minutes (surface sterilization), then put the curd in a clean jar, top up with the hot water, and screw the lid on. Peanut butter jars are approximately the size of one cube; treated in this way and left undisturbed, bean curd will keep about a week.

The second fail-safe method of preservation is freezing. This will preserve flavor but utterly transform texture. Defrosted, the bean curd will be like a sponge (or piece of bread), hence most appropriate for braised and fried dishes but not for steaming. It should be noted that some people actually prefer the substantial, chewy texture of frozen bean curd to the silken custard-like nature of the fresh.

COOKING: Delicate in both taste and texture, fresh bean curd is best used for simple dishes requiring a minimum of manipulation, e.g. steaming, braising, pan-frying, or simmering briefly in soup. As mentioned above, preserved mustard stem goes exceptionally well with it. Use the two together in soups, casseroles, stir-fry dishes, or the simple salad-like combination, *Leung Baan Dau Fu,* described below.

LEUNG BAAN DAU FU
Fresh bean curd
Preserved mustard stem (*za choi* 榨菜), chopped in thin slivers
(Spring onions, chopped)
(Dried shrimp, soaked, chopped)
Soy sauce
Sesame oil and/or roasted sesame seeds

Put the bean curd on the serving plate. Scatter mustard root, spring onions, and shrimp over the top. Drizzle with soy sauce, then sesame oil. Scatter sesame seeds decoratively over all, and serve.

BRAISED BEAN CURD
Pork, shredded, seasoned
Garlic, crushed
1–2 slices fresh ginger, crushed
Bean curd, whole or quartered cubes, fresh or frozen*
Any or all of the following:
    Winter mushrooms, soaked
    Fresh mushrooms
    Bamboo shoots, sliced
    Shallots or spring onions, chopped

In a casserole or saucepan, lightly fry pork with garlic. Add bean curd and brown lightly on all sides. Add ginger, other vegetables, soy sauce, and light stock or water. Cover and braise 10–20 minutes. Adjust seasoning with dashes of sesame oil, white pepper, and soy sauce. Serve as is or, if sauce seems thin, remove solid ingredients to the serving dish, thicken remaining liquid with cornstarch, pour over rest and then serve.

Shanghai variation For variety, modify the above directions slightly and subsequently produce a spicier Shanghai dish known as *Ma Poh Dau Fu* (麻婆豆腐). The modifications are as follows: mince the pork; mash or cut the curd in small cubes; add no other vegetables; use approximately 1 part by volume of pork per 2 parts bean curd, and season with chilli-bean paste (*dau baan laat jeung*). You will need to thicken the dish with cornstarch to create a stiff, almost sauce-like consistency for the entire dish.

Vegetarian variation In place of the pork and garlic, use mushrooms, either whole or minced. Add preserved mustard stem, again, either in chunks, slivers, slices, or minced bits. You may add a few fresh green peas at the end for color.

   * If using frozen bean curd, defrost it. Squeeze out excess water. Then proceed as above, first lightly pan-frying the curd before braising it.

GREENS & BEAN CURD SOUP
Bring water to the boil; flavor with seasoned sliced lean pork or slices of fresh fish (wait, if making miso soup). Carefully add squares of bean curd. Then add greens, such as lettuce (common) or mustard cabbage (recommended for those with flu). Simmer a minute or two until all is cooked. Adjust seasoning and serve.

DEEP-FRIED BEAN CURD   *Dau fu pok* 豆腐卜 ; *Yau dau fu* 油豆腐

APPEARANCE: These are small cubes (*dau fu pok* 豆腐卜) or squares (*yau dau fu* 油豆腐) of bean curd that have been deep-fried. The outer surface is crusty and golden-yellow while the inside is porous.

QUALITY: The freshness of the bean curd and of the oil used for deep-frying are the two main factors critical to quality. The cubes (or squares) should be bright in color without a strong oily odor or feel. Follow the crowd: patronize a shop with a lot of customers, hence a rapid turnover.

COMMENTS: Deep-frying gives this form of bean curd a chewy, crusty texture and adds an oily dimension to its flavor that differs substantially from soft, bland, fresh bean curd. In Chinese nutritional terms, the deep-frying makes it a more 'heating' food, hence more innately balanced (as bean curd is considered 'cooling') and more appropriate for boiling rather than stir-frying. In any case, adding a bit of ginger or pickled vegetable will stimulate digestion of both the curd and its oil.

PREPARATION: Before cooking pour boiling water over them in order to remove excess oil and/or dirt—especially if they came from an open-air market stall.

COOKING: 'Braise or boil' is the imperative from Cantonese kitchens. Soup of *dau fu pok* with fresh fish or fishballs, shreds of pickled mustard root, and mung bean vermicelli is particularly satisfying and refreshing in summer.
For more hearty fare, try the following:

MUSHROOMS & DEEP-FRIED BEAN CURD OVER LETTUCE
Lettuce
Dau fu pok or *yau dau fu*
Mushrooms, either dried and soaked, or fresh; of any sort e.g. button, black, or straw
(Seahair, *faat choi* 髮菜 , soaked and drained)
(Oyster sauce)
Ginger, soy sauce, white pepper

Parboil lettuce and mound on serving dish. In hot oil, fry mushrooms until fragrant, then add pieces of deep-fried bean curd, ginger, and seahair if handy. Toss and cook for 1 minute. Add water or light stock to a depth of 1/2 inch; season with oyster sauce and/or soy sauce and white pepper; cover and simmer 5–10 minutes. When ready to serve, adjust seasoning, thicken sauce with cornstarch, (add a dash of sesame oil for fragrance and gloss), and pour over lettuce.

PRESSED BEAN CURD *Dau fu gon* 豆腐乾

APPEARANCE: This bean curd is square, like the fresh, but only about 1/4 the height of the latter, and more solid (less fragile) because much of the liquid has been pressed out. As illustrated, two types may be found in Chinese markets: a larger (3-inch-square) ivory-colored one, and a smaller (2-inch-square) reddish one. The color of the latter reportedly comes from a coating of five-spice powder (*ng heung fun* 五香粉).

QUALITY: As with fresh bean curd, check the color and smell. The squares, while not shiny, should nevertheless have clear color and a clean, beany smell.

COMMENTS: The important difference between this and fresh bean curd is texture. With less water, the curd is less fragile, and can be cut in slices or shreds, stir-fried or braised. But it also tends to be drier, as the slightly astringent nature of the beans becomes more prominent. For balance, then, cook these with warming condiments (e.g. ginger, garlic) to warm the cool nature of soy beans, and with oil and/or sharp, rich sauces to harmonize the astringency and the blandness.

COOKING:

Western Sliced in shreds, it can be added to bean salads or included in vegetable sautés. This form is particularly suitable as a substitute for *ricotta* cheese in Italian dishes such as *lasagna* and *ravioli*. Think twice, however, before putting bean curd AND dairy products such as cheese in your stomach at the same time. Coming from opposite sides of the globe and opposite ends of the food spectrum, the two are not necessarily compatible.

Chinese Pressed bean curd is most common and most frequently served in northern China. There it is typically combined with other fresh vegetables—cut in shapes to match the veg—and seasoned with chillies, sesame oil, and salt-fermented cabbages, in both hot and cold dishes. Four shapes are possible:

Cut it in **matchstick-shreds** and stir-fry with other shredded ingredients: carrot, kelp, and mung bean sprouts; carrot and celery; scallions and cucumber; green and red peppers; all make good combinations. Or, again cut in matchstick shreds, stir-fry with winter mushrooms, ginger, dried shrimp, and cabbage, then braise with mung bean vermicelli or combine with cooked noodles.

Chop in **cubes** and braise it with pork (meat, kidney, liver), mushrooms, and bamboo shoots, also cut in cubes and seasoned with dark soy sauce. With eight different ingredients and a hefty dollop of chilli, this becomes *Baat Bo Laat Jeung* (八寶辣醬) or 'Eight Treasure Hot Sauce', a popular Shanghai dish.

Or, cut in **broad slices** and stir-fry with pork and white cabbage, also—typically—with chilli sauce.

Finally, left **whole**, it can be smoked over rice and tea leaves, and then used in any of the ways described above.

VEGETARIAN 'EIGHT TREASURES'

Pressed bean curd
Green peppers
Winter mushrooms
Red peppers
Fresh straw mushrooms
Peanuts
Green peas
Scallions
Chilli

Soak the mushrooms; cut in 1/2-inch cubes. Cut bean curd and peppers in 1/2-inch cubes. Parboil straw mushrooms; use them whole if small, or chop if large. For best results, stir-fry these vegetables separately: the winter mushrooms; the green and red pepper together; the bean curd cubes alone. Then combine everything, add chilli and soy sauce for seasoning, and enough water to braise. Cook rather vigorously to blend flavors. When virtually done, add peanuts and scallions, thicken any liquid with cornstarch to create sauce—and dish it up.

N.B. You may also add bamboo shoots, jicama, and/or water chestnuts.

WINTER MELON *Doeng gwa* 冬瓜

APPEARANCE: This is one of the largest vegetables grown. Mature winter melons resemble their cousins, watermelons, in shape but regularly outstrip them in size (10 inch plus in diameter) and in weight (up to 100 lbs). The dark green skin is thin, hard, and waxy—source of their other common name, 'wax gourd'.

In the market, expect to see only part of a whole melon because it is commonly sold by the slice.

QUALITY: Buy slices that have been freshly cut, with firm, white flesh which smells clean.

COMMENTS: Winter melon has nourished Asians since the earliest days of agriculture. This has required a lot of melon because some 95 per cent of it is water. Diners particularly welcome its juicy flesh during hot weather, for reasons that concern its chemistry as well as its high water content.

According to Chinese nutritionists, winter melon is the most effective vegetable for clearing summer heat from the body. Specifically, it is said to promote urination. This can be particularly important in hot weather when excess perspiration may leave too little water and minerals behind to flush out the kidneys properly. Chemical analysis shows winter melon to have exceptionally high amounts of sodium, a vital electrolyte excreted liberally in perspiration. Hence, the mineral-enriched broth of winter melon soup can restore electrolyte balance, help cleanse the kidneys,

reduce edema associated with reduced urination, and sooth sunstroke and thirst. The melon's skin is considered even more medicinally effective than the flesh, hence in summer tonic soups (see below) the whole thing is used, peel, seeds and all.

Use cut pieces of melon soon after purchase or store them in such a way that air can circulate around them because the moist, exposed surfaces will deteriorate and off-flavors travel quickly through the porous flesh.

PREPARATION: This depends entirely on what you plan to cook.

Home-style summer soups call for flesh, skin, and seeds, so you need only rinse and chop. For stir-frying or braising, peel and de-seed. For attempting a Winter Melon Pond, remove seeds and some of the flesh, and carve designs shallowly in the skin.

COOKING:

Western Your best bet is to make soup. Use it fearlessly in large quantities, add other vegetables (carrot, celery, onion) and/or meats or bones (preferably pork or chicken), and simmer the whole business for at least an hour for best results.

Or, like any summer squash, winter melon may be sautéed, steamed, braised, or baked. Results tend to be watery, soft, and bland, calling for compensation in the form of heavy seasoning (e.g. herbs) in the pot or hearty companions (e.g. ham, curry) on the table.

Chinese The Cantonese invariably make soup with this and consume it often, with relief and relish, during sultry weather. Herbalists and supermarkets sell a measured assortment of dried ingredients that go in with the melon to enhance its beneficial effects: barley, lablab beans, hyacinth beans, adzuki beans, dried kapok flowers, lotus seed pods, and the pith of a sedge. (N.B. Pork is optional but usually added as well, primarily for flavor).

Alternatively, winter melon can be cooked like fuzzy melon, i.e. stir-fried, steamed, or braised. In restaurants, soup is served in the melon—rather than vice versa—as the elaborate and famous Winter Melon Pond (*Doeng Gwa Joeng* 冬瓜盅). The melon typically arrives in a silver tureen, its waxy skin decoratively carved with auspicious motifs such as dragons and phoenixes, and its central cavity filled with a rich broth and assorted diced ingredients.

The main principle in making any soup with winter melon is to use a lot of winter melon—virtually equal volumes water and melon. A wide variety of accompaniments can be used to flavor the broth, e.g.:

Pork, meat or bones, and winter mushrooms
Barbecued duck (*siu ngaap* 燒鴨), meat and bones
Dried shrimp (*ha mai* 蝦米), soaked and fried lightly in oil, plus mung bean vermicelli
 (*fun see* 粉絲), soaked
Ham shreds and fresh mushrooms
Chicken, meat or bones
Salted duck egg (*haam daan* 鹹蛋)
Adzuki beans, barley, mung beans, a strip of kelp
Soy bean sprouts, strip of kelp, and—at the last minute—shreds of preserved mustard stem
 (*za choi* 搾菜)

N.B. For a miniature version of Winter Melon Pond, see recipe with bottle gourd (p 80).

FUZZY MELON *Cheet gwa* 節瓜

APPEARANCE: This melon might be mistaken for a cucumber or a courgette except for skin texture (hairy), color (blotchy), and shape (broader than the former two, and slightly swollen at each end like a dumbbell). The average specimen measures 4–8 inches in length and 2–3 inches in diameter.

QUALITY: The smaller and younger they are the firmer and more uniform the flesh.

COMMENTS: Fuzzy melon is a diminutive race of the gigantic winter melon. Like the British vegetable marrow and the American zucchini, it is bland in flavor with a fine-grained texture that softens quickly and readily absorbs flavors in cooking.

The nutritional qualities of fuzzy melon seem equally unexceptional. It is considered mildly cooling and easily digested, particularly appropriate for summer dishes and suitable for all ages. As one Chinese doctor describes it, fuzzy melon is 'the most neutral vegetable... suitable for consumption year-round to clear toxic heat in all internal organs.'

PREPARATION: Wash; peel. For steaming, halve. For stir-frying or braising, chop in thick strips (1/4-inch diameter and 2 inches long).

COOKING:

Western Of all of the Chinese vegetable melons or summer squashes, this is the one that most resembles courgettes/zucchini/vegetable marrow. Bland but not necessarily boring, think of it as the perfect raw material for creative cooking. It may be steamed, boiled, braised, sautéed, baked, pickled, stuffed with minced meat and/or vegetables, or simply eaten raw. Capitalize on its sponge-like character by seasoning it subtly with herbs or richly with cheese, nuts, or seeds. Imagination is perhaps the most important ingredient in preparing this vegetable tastefully.

Chinese Abundant in the markets and versatile in the kitchen, fuzzy melon is a staple from spring through autumn in Cantonese home cooking. It is steamed, braised, boiled, and/or stir-fried—with chicken, beef, pork, fish, and/or other vegetables and/or dried foods. When stir-fried alone, add ginger, spring onions, and stock for flavor. If you choose to mix it with other ingredients, consider these combinations: shrimp and spring onions; beef and oyster sauce; pork and mushrooms; cashew nuts and green peas or pea pods; ham or carrots and black mushrooms.

FUN SEE & FUZZY MELON SOUP

Lean pork, thinly sliced and seasoned
1 fuzzy melon, peeled and chopped in sticks
1 salted duck egg (*haam daan* 鹹蛋)
2–3 winter mushrooms (*doeng gwu* 冬菇), soaked
1 handful mung bean vermicelli (*fun see* 粉絲)
Ginger

Bring 5–6 cups of water with crushed slice of ginger, pork, mushrooms, and mushroom-soaking liquid to a boil. Simmer until broth is well-flavored, about 30 minutes. Cut vermicelli into shorter, more manageable (i.e. 4–5-inch) lengths, then add to the broth. Meanwhile, rinse black powder off the egg and crack it directly into the soup while stirring vigorously to break the egg white into fine shreds. Continue to simmer the soup a few minutes while adjusting the seasoning; serve.

MULTIFARIOUS MELON & MUSHROOMS

This combination offers unlimited variations:

(1) Stir-fried. Use winter mushrooms, wood ear mushrooms (*wun yee*), or fresh. You may add onions; and/or dried shrimp (soaked); and/or meat or fish. To cook, in the wok, fry mushrooms lightly until fragrant. Add melon, toss, sprinkle with salt, cast in shreds or a crushed slice of ginger, add a splash of water to create steam, cover, and cook a minute or two; dish. Then—if so planned—stir-fry any meat, return the veg, toss to mix, adjust seasoning, and serve.

(2) Boiled. Use meat or bones; or soy beans or soy bean sprouts. Combine all, with a crushed slice of ginger, and simmer until broth is flavored.

(3) Steamed. Wash and peel melon; cut in half lengthwise. Cut mushrooms in thin shreds, toss with soy sauce, dash of pepper, and a little oil. Place melons on steaming dish, cut sides up. Cover with a single layer of mushrooms. Steam until melon is tender. Serve as is, or—more elaborately—make a sauce with mushroom-soaking liquid, soy sauce, and cornstarch, pour over, then garnish with minced spring onions.

(4) Stuffed. Prepare a minced stuffing—pork, onions, mushrooms, shrimp; or soy beans, carrot, mushrooms, onions; etc—and season it well with salt or soy sauce and a little oil. Cut melon in half cross-wise and hollow out the center. Dust inner surface lightly with cornstarch to help the stuffing stick. You may include some of the melon's innards with the minced filling. Then stuff melons.

In saucepan, brown melons briefly on all sides. Add a little water or stock and a bit of ginger, cover, and braise until tender, 15–30 minutes. Occasionally turn the melons so they cook evenly and add water to prevent burning.

When done, remove melons to serving dish and slice into 1/2- inch, bite-sized rounds. Season the liquid remaining in the pan, then thicken it with cornstarch into a sauce that you finally pour over the melon slices; serve.

BOTTLE GOURD

APPEARANCE: The bottle gourd species produces fruit in a remarkable spectrum of shape and size, but the skin is the same: smooth, tough, and most commonly light green. Two marketed versions are:

Wu lo gwa (葫蘆瓜): Illustrated below.
Po gwa (蒲瓜): Long and thin, straight or curved, and generally 12–30 inches long.

QUALITY: As with other vegetable melons, select smaller younger ones in the expectation that they will be more tender and sweeter.

GENERAL COMMENTS: Tighter than a sealed drum, more durable than a plastic bag, cheaper than tupperware, this gourd is believed to have floated from Africa, its native home, to South America, where it was growing by 7000–5000 BC. Later varieties, perhaps even more seaworthy, eventually reached Asia, where they have been grown and eaten or dried and used as receptacles ever since. Indeed, in China, the *wu lo gwa* is legendary. Ancient art inevitably portrays sages and monks with a gourd or two dangling from their belts, transporting water or herbs. The term *wu lo* (葫蘆) has no other meaning than to describe the shape of this particular vegetable.

Today, this gourd seems more common in paintings than on dinner tables—perhaps regrettably. It has the same basic attributes of other Chinese summer melons (e.g. fuzzy melon, winter melon), namely white flesh, mild flavor, and diuretic and cooling properties, with an exceptionally fine-grained texture.

PREPARATION: To use a *wu lo* gourd whole as a receptacle for soup or stuffing, slice it open—either crosswise at the neck for soup, or lengthwise for baking with stuffing—scrape out the spongy pith with seeds, then proceed as directed or desired.

For other uses, these gourds must be peeled.

COOKING:

Western Prepare as you would summer squash. For novelty, bake the *wu lo* variety whole or halved with a filling of seasoned minced meats, vegetables, and rice as a meal in itself.

Chinese Either variety may be boiled in soup or stir-fried in any of the ways described for fuzzy melon. In addition, the hard skin, bowl shape, and diminutive size of the *wu lo* gourd make it an ideal receptacle for soup cooked in the style of Winter Melon Pond on a household scale (see below).

Wu Lo Gwa Joeng

Ingredients:
1 mature *wu lo gwa*
Any or all of the following in quantities to taste:
    Meat, cooked and thinly sliced: chicken, pork, ham, dried duck, etc.
    Winter mushrooms, soaked, whole or sliced
    Straw mushrooms
    Bamboo shoots
    Spring onions
    Lotus seeds (*leen jee* 蓮子)
    Shrimp, fresh or dried, soaked (*ha mai* 蝦米)
Chicken stock or water

Equipment:
Heatproof dish with high, sloping sides to support gourd
Small dish or plate to cover the top of gourd
Pot larger than the heatproof dish

Procedure:
Slice gourd open at the neck between the bulges. Scoop out seeds and spongy flesh of the central cavity, leaving at least 1 inch (or as much as possible) of melon towards the outside.

Place melon on supporting dish inside the pot; the rim of the dish must not cut into the melon or the latter will collapse as it softens during cooking. Put ingredients into melon with stock or water to fill approximately 2/3 full. Cover top of gourd with small dish. Add boiling water to just below the lip of the supporting dish; cover entire pot with its lid. Bring to a boil and simmer gently until melon is cooked, 1–2 hours. Check occasionally and replenish water as necessary. The melon is cooked when its flesh is soft and transparent; avoid overcooking lest the whole thing collapse.

When done, adjust soup's flavor with salt and white pepper. Serve either directly from the gourd, scraping melon from the sides with each ladle-full of soup, or from a tureen, pouring soup in first and then scraping melon in last.

YELLOW CUCUMBER   *Wong gwa* 黄瓜

APPEARANCE: 'Yellow torpedo' would be a more descriptive name for this vegetable. An average individual measures 10–15 inches in length, 4–5 inches in diameter, and 1–2 pounds in weight. The skin has a coarse netted texture, reminiscent of a cantaloupe.

QUALITY: For eating raw, choose smaller—hopefully younger—ones in which the flesh should be more tender. For soup, select large mature melons.

COMMENTS: Predictably enough, this melon has the same characteristics of crisp flesh and cool taste as ordinary cucumbers. For eating raw, green cucumbers are preferred, being more tender, tastier, and crisp. For boiling soup the yellow cucumber is preferred because it withstands cooking better and yields a better flavor to the broth. For stir-frying and braising, either will do.

Even though yellow and green cucumbers may seem virtually identical in terms of genetics and chemistry, in terms of Chinese nutrition they are distinct. The yellow version is considered to be particularly effective in helping the body cope with dry weather—alleviating dry cough and generally moisturizing the lungs.

PREPARATION: For eating raw, peel, remove seeds, and slice as desired. For use in soup, scrub well and chop in chunks (use both peel and seeds).

COOKING:
Western Substitute yellow cucumbers for green in any recipe except those calling for green skin; this one definitely needs to be peeled. Use it raw, boiled, braised, stir-fried, or pickled.
Chinese In China, most of the crop becomes a sweet pickle known as *cha gwa* (茶瓜), which is used in soup (see page 25), on steamed fish, or in sweet-and-sour sauces. In Hong Kong, most of the yellow cucumbers sold in the markets go into soup. The entire melon is used, seeds, skin, and all.

YELLOW CUCUMBER SOUP
1 yellow cucumber, scrubbed and chopped (about 3 lb)
1 lb pork bones or 1/2 lb lean pork
2 Peking dates (*mut jo* 蜜棗)
1/4 dried tangerine peel (*gwoh pei* 菓皮)
1 tbsp Chinese almonds/apricot kernels (*naam but hung* 南北杏)

Combine all ingredients in large pot with 2–3 times as much water. Boil for at least two hours, reducing liquid by one third to one half. Season with salt and serve.

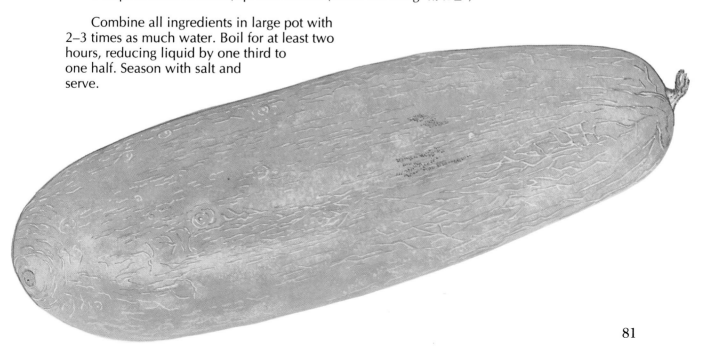

CHAYOTE   *Haap jeung gwa* 合掌瓜 ; *Faat sau gwa* 佛手瓜

APPEARANCE: This vegetable has more names than a cat has lives, and each name helps identify it. It is called 'vegetable pear' because the stem end is narrower than the base; it is called 'mango squash' because it grows on a vine like a squash but has a single, large, flat, oval seed rather than the typical cucurbit-type cavity of small hard-shelled seeds. Both Cantonese names evoke religious images: *haap jeung* means Christian hands in prayer, while *faat sau* means Buddha's hand. Chayote is an American Indian rendition of the original Latin American name; choko seems to be the Australian rendition of chayote.

In any case, these melons are usually pale green to white, with a smooth or sparsely spiny, somewhat furrowed skin. They vary in length, up to about 8 inches, and will feel rather heavy for their size should you pick one up.

QUALITY: Select firm, unblemished specimens, the smaller the more tender. Large ones yield more flesh for the time spent peeling; tiny ones (i.e. 2–3 inches) need no peeling at all.

COMMENTS: The chayote is an old South American vegetable, the fruit of a perennial vine that grows quickly and is completely edible—roots, shoots, leaves, and fruits (both flesh and seeds). No wonder it is now grown in most warm climates from Asia to the Americas. Its flesh is white, fine-textured, and mild-flavored. The large central seed is also edible, and tender, though disappointingly bland compared to the rich delight of squash and pumpkin seeds.

Nutritionally speaking, chayote offers little to shout about. Western analyses show relatively meagre amounts of vitamins and minerals. The Chinese are mum, but pale color and melon family membership suggest it has cooling properties. As with prayer, perhaps benefits become apparent only after steady consumption over time...

PREPARATION: Wash. For using the cooked flesh, boil in the skin. For other purposes, peel. Admittedly, this task is tedious because the surface undulates into crevices, but it is necessary because the skin does not soften in cooking.

COOKING:
Western This is edible raw. And in this condition, like carrots, its firm, fine-grained texture and thick flesh make it suitable for a range of chopping options. Cut into matchsticks and serve with dips; shred and toss in salads; slice thinly and marinate with other vegetables in an oil-vinegar dressing.

Chayote is equally amenable to cooking. Steam, boil, bake, braise, or fry it. Its firm texture withstands stir-fry tossing and/or long-cooking admirably, while its mild flavor readily absorbs and complements other flavors.

Chinese The Cantonese recommend boiling chayote with pork of some sort—meat or bones—in soup.

It is also good for stir-frying or braising. Follow any of the suggestions for fuzzy melon, particularly those involving richly flavored companions (winter mushrooms; five-spice beef; deep-fried bean curd; etc).

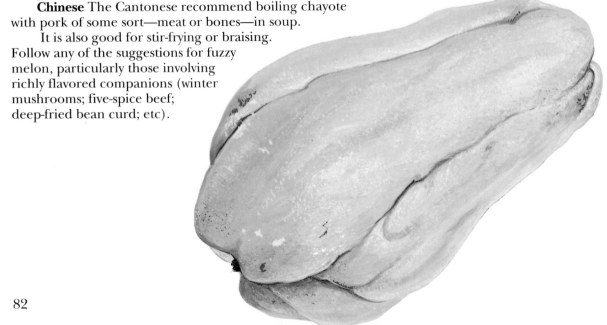

ANGLED LUFFA *See gwa* 絲瓜

APPEARANCE: Identify this vegetable—a melon, in fact—by its prominent, longitudinal ridges and exceptional length. Individuals usually measure 1–2 inches in diameter, 1–2 feet in length.

QUALITY: Select young ones, which will be dark green in color, thin, resilient, and preferably long. To test resilience, grasp a prospective purchase by the stem end, lift, and waft gently. If young it will bounce slightly; if old it will be as stiff as a broom handle. Stiffness is not itself a problem; it is the bitterness associated with old age that you want to avoid.

COMMENTS: This luffa, as well as the sponge-making one (see p 85) are old Chinese crops. Farmers favor it because the mother plant tolerates hot humid weather; diners enjoy it for its sweet flavor and unusual texture. When cooked, the central flesh goes spongy while the skin remains dark green and crisp—nice contrasts for both the eye and the tongue.
Though common in vegetable markets today, in the past luffa was thought of more as medicine than (innocuous) vegetable, too 'cold' in energy for daily consumption. At least one Chinese doctor disagrees; he maintains that luffa is neutral, and suggests that its 'cold' reputation comes from undercooking, which would leave certain alkaline substances present to irritate the gastro-intestinal tract. Well-cooked luffa should be simply cooling and moisturizing, a valuable aid in tolerating summer heat. If in doubt and for maximum pleasure at the table, add something 'warm' (e.g. ginger, onions) at the beginning of cooking, and let it linger a bit on the heat.

PREPARATION: With a vegetable peeler or small knife remove the ridges. If the melon is young, leave the skin between the ridges intact, creating stripes. If it is old and the skin very leathery, remove it altogether as it can be unpalatably bitter. For stir-frying, create wedge-shaped pieces by chopping diagonally but rolling the melon a quarter-turn between chops.

COOKING:
Western Steam, boil, or sauté as you would courgettes or summer squash; season with herbs, grated cheese, or simply butter, salt, and pepper.

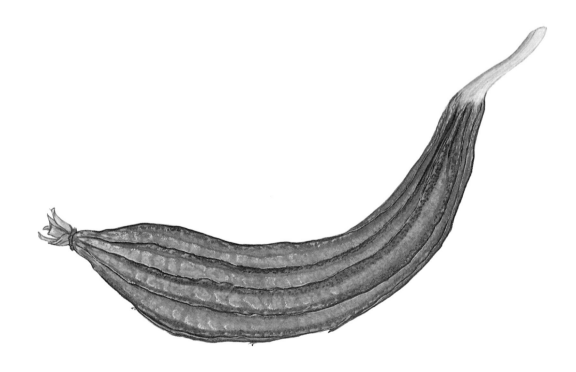

Chinese Generally, Hong Kong Cantonese stir-fry this one, though Chinese elsewhere recommend it for soup. Virtually any of the combinations suggested for fuzzy melon work equally well here. Meat (pork, beef, or chicken) and another vegetable, such as onions, spring onions, winter mushrooms, wood's ear mushrooms, or fresh straw mushrooms, plus angled luffa, are compatible. The most typical Cantonese combination is given below.

ANGLED LUFFA IN CONCERT

2 angled luffas, approximately 2 feet long
1 onion
Wood's ear mushrooms (*wun yee* 云耳), soaked (making about 1 rice-bowl-full when
    rehydrated)
Ginger
(Fresh fish, sliced)

If using fish, marinate it with a dash of wine, a bit of grated ginger, and pinches of salt and white pepper. Prepare the luffa as described above, chopping in wedges. Cut the onion in wedges, then separate them into layers. Pick over the mushrooms individually to remove any bits of wood clinging to their 'feet'.

First, if using fish, stir-fry it quickly over high heat until just barely cooked; set aside. Then, stir-fry the onion. When fragrant and beginning to soften (but still crunchy), add the melon, and a slice or two of crushed ginger; toss; season with salt. Add the mushrooms, a bit of water to create steam, then cover and cook until done. Remove the lid, return the fish, toss to heat through, and serve.

SPONGE LUFFA *Soi gwa* 水瓜

APPEARANCE: These are dark green melons of the same dumbbell shape as a fuzzy melon but fatter, often only twice as long as broad. Their skin is rough and marked with wide-spaced, dark stripes running from stem to base. They often reach market with a shrivelled flower still attached at one end.

QUALITY: Select unblemished fruits, the smaller and younger the better.

COMMENTS: This is the fruit whence cometh luffa sponges. To produce a sponge, fruits are left to mature on the vine; as they mature, the flesh becomes tough and fibrous. When thoroughly dry the skin is peeled away and the seeds removed from the central cavities, leaving the tough scratchy sponge of commerce.

But one vine can produce more luffas than a man needs sponges, so much of the crop is harvested young and sent to the market for food. To a botanist, this explains why these melons often have flowers still attached, i.e. all melons—and squash, for that matter—originally bear flowers that eventually drop off after pollination. The closer to pollination a fruit is harvested, the more likely the flower will still be *in situ*.

Nutritionally, sponge luffa has the characteristics of the angled luffa: cooling and moisturizing, with a yen for pungent condiments and a need to be well cooked.

PREPARATION: Wash; slice.

COOKING:
Western Steam, boil, or sauté and season as you would any summer squash. Cook it well, and season with something aromatic (e.g. pepper, ginger, onions) for delectable results. The porous texture will collapse and shrink as it cooks, so prepare quantities and plan serving style accordingly.

Chinese The Cantonese recommend this for soup. Simmer it for hours, with pork bones or meat. Or toss it into quick vegetable soups—using carrot, spring onions, ginger and/or preserved mustard stem (*za choi* 搾菜) for balance and contrast.

BITTER MELON *Fu gwa* 苦瓜

APPEARANCE: Corrugated skin earmarks this vegetable; it varies in color from deep green to almost white (having been blanched on the vine). Typical specimens measure 4–5 inches long, although there are miniatures barely 2 inches and behemoths up to 10 inches in length.

QUALITY: In general, select firm, small melons in hopes that they will be crisp and less bitter. Larger, ripe melons—identified by bright red seeds inside—tend to be softer and more bitter.

COMMENTS: Indians curry it; Sri Lankans pickle it; Indonesians serve it in salads. Throughout the Asian tropics, it is ... bitter. For some palates this is an unforgivable sin. For those educated in Asian nutritional theory, however, it is a valuable virtue, since bitterness is considered one of the fundamental flavors essential to a balanced diet.

This melon is an example *sans pareil* of bitterness, which is synonymous with 'cold' energy and strong powers of detoxification. Indeed, eating bitter melon is said to cleanse the blood and improve the condition of the liver, with immediate benefits to the eyes and skin. Chinese mothers routinely serve it to teenagers suffering from acne and to those who develop pimples after eating seafood—both signs of a system trying to cleanse itself of toxins. But bitterness can depress the stomach. Hence, sugar (to stimulate the stomach) and warming condiments such as garlic, chillies, and meat are natural companions for this potential vegetable pariah.

PREPARATION: The two keys to preparing bitter melon palatably are pre-treatment and sweet seasoning; both will blunt the cutting edge of its bitterness. The common methods of pre-treatment are:
  (1) Blanching. Wash the melon well; halve lengthwise; remove and discard seeds. Bring water to a rolling boil, drop melon halves in; when melon turns bright in color, drain, and rinse to stop cooking.
  (2) Salting. Wash; halve; remove seeds and pith. Leave whole or slice, as recipe dictates. Place in large bowl, sprinkle with salt (preferably coarse), about 1 teaspoon per melon, and toss lightly; let stand 15–20 minutes. As with salting cucumbers, liquid will accumulate and the melon will soften. Rinse if desired to remove excess salt; squeeze dry.

COOKING:
Western As with bitter greens, sauté slices—possibly with chopped bacon—and season with a healthy pinch of sugar, a dash of vinegar, and sprinkle of salt and pepper.
Chinese The Cantonese enjoy this vegetable in a multitude of ways, generally paired with something rich (e.g. eggs, beef, eel) to balance the potentially debilitating coolness of too much bitterness. Hence, bitter melon is recommended: stir-fried in omelettes; stir-fried with beef; stuffed with minced fish and braised in black bean sauce (see below); or boiled in soup with eel or pork. For vegetarian dishes, select rich (e.g. deep-fried bean curd) and sweet (e.g. squash) and warm (e.g. garlic, onions, chillies) companions.

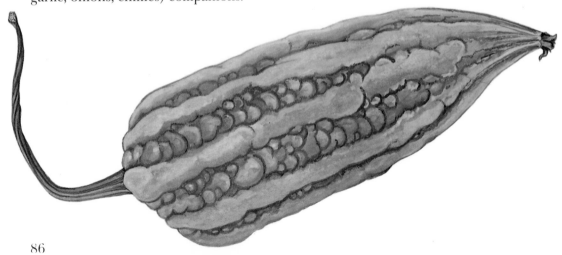

STUFFED BITTER MELON

Bitter melon, washed, halved, and seeded
Fish meat, minced
Fermented black beans (*dau see* 豆豉)
Garlic

Season fish with grated ginger, salt, white pepper, a dash of oil, and a bit of cornstarch; stir well to make a stiff and homogenous paste. Blanch bitter melon; drain. When cool enough to handle chop into large squares. Dust inner surface with cornstarch, then spread with fish paste.

Mash together equal parts minced garlic and fermented black beans, using 1–2 teaspoons of each per bitter melon. In a shallow pan, sauté garlic-black bean paste, then add stuffed melon squares. Brown on both sides. Add a little each of water, soy sauce, and sugar; cover and braise until cooked, 5–10 minutes. Remove to serving dish. Heat juices remaining in pan to the boil, adjust seasoning, add cornstarch paste to thicken and a bit of sesame oil to enrich it, then pour over cooked squares.

HOT DRY-FRIED BITTER MELON

Bitter melon
Chillies
Fermented black beans (*dau see* 豆豉)
Ginger
Spring onions

Prepare the bitter melon as described above, preferably using the salting method; squeeze dry. Seed and chop the chillies. Rinse the black beans. Chop the spring onions in two just above the white bulbs; chop the greens in 1-inch lengths. Mince the bulbs, then mash together with the black beans. You are ready to cook.

Heat the wok without oil. Add the bitter melon; toss and cook over high heat until it is limp, dry, and fragrant. Remove. Now add oil, the ginger, black bean mash, chilli, spring onion greens (in that order). Stir to mix; there should be enough oil to give everything a bright sheen. Return the bitter melon; season with a pinch of sugar and dash of soy sauce. Cook to the desired degree; serve.

SQUASH   *Naam gwa* 南瓜

APPEARANCE: In America, this vegetable comes in a great range of colors, shapes, and sizes, but in Asia, two varieties seem to prevail. One is plain brown as illustrated here; the other is orange-brown with irregular dark green stripes. Both have bright orange flesh, measure 4–10 inches in diameter or length, and can be either round (the Japanese pumpkin) or variously elongated.

QUALITY: Check the skin for worm holes and bruises. Check the stem end for rot, and for the presence of a stem. Fully mature squash fall cleanly off the vine—and will have the sweetest, most tender flesh.

COMMENTS: Winter squashes are native to the Americas, and have only relatively recently migrated to Asia. Although becoming more popular, they have a long way to go to usurp the most-favored flavor status that white-fleshed summer cooking melons enjoy, at least in Canton. As one Hong Kong diner expressed it, 'There is a peculiar taste and [an association with pig food] that prevents it from being on higher tables.' Chinese doctors cast further aspersions on an otherwise tasty vegetable by recommending both flesh and seeds as a good remedy for expelling worms from the intestines.

Associations aside, the flesh of fully mature winter squash is tender, smooth, sweet, flavorful, and rich in vitamin A. Its sweetness warms the body, and stimulates the spleen and stomach—and responds nicely to a twist of lemon in any dish. Its texture is porous, which has a number of implications for the cook. First, baking and sautéing (rather than boiling) develop its flavor better; even purée (for soup, pie, or custard) made from squash that has been first sautéed or baked will seem more robust. Second, when overcooked it is mushy, so watch carefully and manipulate gently as it approaches that stage. Third, beans (astringent) and spices (aromatic), both drying by nature, are good accompaniments.

A whole, mature winter squash can keep for at least a month in the refrigerator.

PREPARATION: Cut open; this could be challenging because the rind could—indeed should—be smooth and quite hard. Remove seeds* and fibrous strings from the central cavity. Leave as halves for baking; or peel, then chop in chunks for braising, or in matchsticks for stir-frying or sautéing.

*The seeds may be eaten separately, either raw (as a vermifuge) or cooked (for pleasure). Separate them from the fibres, rinse, and salt lightly if desired; then either dry-roast in the wok or slow-roast in the oven.

COOKING:

Western Halves may be baked whole, plain, or with any of a variety of fillings (e.g. sausage; apples and raisins; butter and brown sugar). Pieces may be steamed, baked, boiled, braised, or sautéed; they may be served simply as is, buttered with salt and pepper, or further fashioned into custard, pie, or croquettes. The best 'pumpkin' pie is actually and traditionally made from the tastiest squash available, which is not and probably never has been the Halloween-pumpkin variety.

Chinese The Cantonese generally cook this as they do their other orange-fleshed starchy vegetables and, less commonly, as they do their summer melons. Thus, it can be boiled like sweet potatoes to make a sweet soup, or like papaya with pork or fish to make savory soup. Alternatively, it can be stir-fried like fuzzy melon, with chicken, or pork, or pork, onions, and mushrooms, etc. Two examples are given below; the second, squash with bitter melon, provides a superb and satisfying balance of bitter and sweet.

CHICKEN NOODLE SQUASH
In proportions to taste:
Chicken meat
Chicken liver
Squash
Spring onions
Rice vermicelli (or spaghetti)
Ginger, a slice, crushed or cut in fine shreds
Garlic, crushed

Chop chicken meat and liver in shreds. Chop squash in matchsticks, and spring onions in 1-inch lengths.

Cook vermicelli in boiling water until just tender; drain; toss with a little cooked oil to keep them separate.

With hot oil in wok, fry squash, stir, and toss until beginning to cook, add ginger, season with salt, sprinkle with water, cover, and steam until almost tender; remove. Again heat wok with oil, fry garlic until fragrant and discard. Cook chicken; when almost done, add liver, stir and toss, return squash with spring onions as well as noodles. Cook and toss; adjust seasoning and serve.

BRAISED BITTERSWEET MEDLEY
Squash
Bitter melon
Garlic
Fermented black beans (*dau see* 豆豉)
Spring onions, chopped in 1-inch lengths

Halve, seed, slice, and salt bitter melon (q.v.); let rest 10–20 minutes while it exudes some of its bitterness; drain and squeeze. Meanwhile, chop squash in cubes, using about twice as much squash as melon. Use approximately equal amounts of garlic and black beans, and about 1 teaspoon of each for 2 cups (total) of the vegetables. Mash garlic and black beans together.

In a casserole, heat oil, fry garlic-black bean mash until fragrant. Add squash, then melon. Toss to mix well; season with light (and dark, if handy) soy sauce(s), add a bit of water, cover, and braise over low heat until squash is cooked. Toss in spring onions. When ready to serve, thicken any liquid remaining with cornstarch to make a sauce, and dot with a bit of sesame oil if fragrance and shine are desired.

BELL PEPPER *Cheng jiu* 青椒

APPEARANCE: Distinguish mild bell peppers from their fiery cousins by size and shape. These measure 3–4 inches in height and diameter.

QUALITY: Select firm, unblemished fruits. Check stem end for signs of rot. Those slightly red are beginning to ripen and should have more vitamin C and sweetness.

COMMENTS: The bell pepper is a derivative of the chilli and a second-cousin of the tomato and eggplant. All enjoy international popularity because the plants grow quickly, fruit prolifically, and respond readily to horticultural manipulation. They therefore reach markets and supermarkets virtually year-round.

Green peppers are not a traditional Chinese food; hence they are not a staple in home-cooking and do not figure in the gastronomic *materia medica*. By extrapolation from the characteristics of the chilli, one can expect green peppers to have the same, albeit mild, superficial warming effect of chillies (i.e. warming the periphery while cooling the core by stimulating blood circulation). Thus, true warmth balances green peppers, and improves their digestion: e.g. cooking them; combining them with garlic or aromatic spices; or letting them ripen on the vine (to red). Along these same lines, the intense heat of roasting and frying seems to enhance the flavor and digestibility of peppers, more so than boiling.

PREPARATION: Wash, stem, seed, and chop as desired.

COOKING:
Western Western styles of cooking bell peppers have mostly evolved in South America and in southern European countries. Peppers are useful in small quantities to season casseroles, or in larger pieces and larger proportions as a side dish. They may be roasted, sautéed, steamed, stuffed, braised, or, most simply, tossed raw in salad.

Chinese As mentioned above, bell peppers are a relatively new arrival to China; they permeate Cantonese restaurant cuisine but make only sporadic appearances on home dinner tables. Most commonly they are either stir-fried or deep-fried, as squares spread with a paste of minced fish or pork. Stir-fry mixtures are of two forms: either with fermented black beans and garlic, or in sweet and sour sauce. The latter generally involves some sort of animal protein (pork, beef, squid), of which the most famous is Sweet & Sour Pork.

PEPPERED BEAN CURD IN SESAME SAUCE

Fresh bean curd
Bell peppers, preferably green and red
Sesame paste
Spring onions
Sesame oil
(Chilli)

Chop the bean curd in small cubes. Similarly, chop the peppers in small squares, and the spring onions in 1-inch lengths. Mix the sesame paste with equal amounts of water and half as much soy sauce (using about 1 tablespoon of paste per 2 squares of bean curd) to make a sauce.

In the wok, over strong heat, stir-fry the peppers until barely cooked; remove. Again heat the wok, add the squares of bean curd and cook until heated through. Return the pepper squares, plus the spring onions; then add the sauce. Simmer a few moments. If the sauce appears too thin, thicken it with cornstarch paste. In any case, drizzle in a bit of sesame oil for fragrance, toss once more for luck, and serve.

STUFFED PEPPER SQUARES

Bell peppers*, cut in 1–2-inch squares
Stuffing:
  Minced seasoned shrimp (as described for Deep-Fried Eggplant, p 94)

Dust the inside of the pepper squares with cornstarch; spread each with stuffing.

Heat oil in wok; lightly brown the filled side of the pepper squares. Flip; fry lightly, then add a little water, a pinch of sugar, soy sauce to taste, chillies or chilli sauce if desired; cover and simmer gently 5–10 minutes. Remove pepper squares to serving dish. Adjust seasoning of sauce, thicken with cornstarch, and pour over the squares.

*Slices of eggplant, pieces of bean curd, and even pieces of bitter melon (for the brave) may be stuffed similarly and cooked together with the peppers.

EGGPLANT *Ngai gwa* 矮瓜

APPEARANCE: Don't let differences in shape and color mislead you; all eggplants have a thin, smooth, waxy skin, rounded base, and leathery 5-pointed leaf-cap enclosing the stem end. In its country of origin, the fruit seldom measures more than 2 inches long, is actually egg-shaped, and may be purple, green, yellow, or white. Varieties cultivated in the West are comparatively and typically huge (8–10 inches long, 4–6 inches in diameter), tear-drop shaped, and purple. Varieties cultivated in the East are more modest in size (5–8 inches long, only 1–2 inches in diameter), cylindrical in shape, and white, pale green, or purple in color.

QUALITY: Select young, smooth, firm, unblemished fruits. Avoid older ones in which seeds will have developed, and shrivelling ones in which flavor and texture will be inferior.

COMMENTS: Alias aubergine in Europe, alias *brinjal* in India, eggplant can be terrible or terrific. Understanding certain of its inalienable characteristics helps ensure delectable results. First, eggplants benefit from preprandial processing—either salting or scorching (see below) in order to transform objectionable flavors. Second, eggplant absorbs oil like a sponge. Thus more oil is needed in cooking it, and slightly acid foods such as tomatoes or vinegared sauces, complement it and that extra oil nicely. Thirdly, length of cooking time greatly affects final texture: cooked quickly at high temperatures, slices absorb flavors but remain thick and succulent; cooked longer they become thin and limp.

In terms of Chinese nutritional theory, eggplant suffers from the Jekyll-and-Hyde syndrome. Theory describes it as calming and cooling; yet on the dinner table it may be accused of being 'hot and damp'. Cooking techniques explain the transformation. Frying warms its innate coldness, but excess oil generates heat and dampness, especially for the liver. Garlic and spices can disperse the damp, while acidic companions can stimulate the liver to metabolize the oils. *Voilà*: East or West, chefs know that eggplant needs something rich, something spicy or pungent, and something acidic to be at its best.

PREPARATION: Wash. To pretreat by scorching, hold it over a naked flame or under a grill until the skin is completely charred. To pretreat by salting, first peel it, if and as desired, then slice, sprinkle with salt (preferably coarse), and let rest 10–15 minutes. Rinse, squeeze, and pat dry.

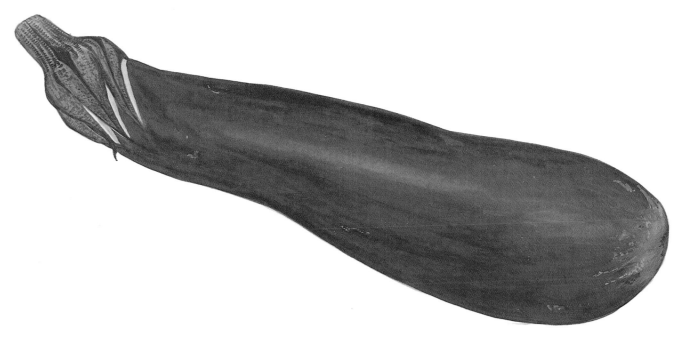

COOKING:

Western Every cuisine that includes eggplant seems to feature it in some classic dish, e.g. Indian *brinjal bhartha*; Greek *moussaka*; Italian *melanzana alla parmigiana*; French *ratatouille*; Middle Eastern *baba ganoush*. In summary, Western cooks sauté, bake, or braise eggplant, sliced or mashed, typically with spices or garlic, cheese or meat.

Chinese Consistent with cuisines elsewhere, the Chinese usually cook eggplant richly: stuffed and deep-fried, braised with pork *en casserole*, or—for a quick homely dish—steamed and mashed with sesame or peanut butter (recipe below).

AUBER-SESAME

Eggplant(s)
Sesame paste (i.e. *tahini*) or peanut butter
Light soy sauce
Cooked peanut oil
(Chopped chillies or chilli sauce)
For garnish: Paprika or chilli powder
               Parsley or coriander

Score eggplant(s) lengthwise 3–4 times. If time permits, salt for 10 minutes, then squeeze dry. Steam until cooked (N.B. Some Cantonese simply lay the eggplant on top of cooking rice.) Meanwhile, combine sauce ingredients according to taste. When eggplant is done, serve in either of the following ways:
(1)   Slice it in bite-size chunks on a dish; pour sauce over or serve separately for dipping.
(2)   Mash eggplant together with sauce until homogenous.
Either way, garnish with a sprig of green (coriander, parsley), and dust with chilli or paprika to brighten its unfortunately drab appearance.

DEEP-FRIED STUFFED EGGPLANT

Stuffing:
1 cup minced fresh fish; or minced lean pork; or shrimp paste as described below;
5–6 dried shrimp, soaked and minced
2 spring onions or shallots, minced
1 tsp cornstarch

Combine these ingredients with salt and white pepper to taste. To improve the final texture of the filling, form it into a ball and throw it onto the counter several times.

Shrimp Paste:
Clean the shrimp. Mash—do not chop—them, either with a spoon and bowl, with a rolling pin and plastic bag, or with the broadside of a cleaver crushing them on a chopping board. Scrape the paste into a bowl, season with salt, white pepper, cornstarch and, if desirable and available, dashes of wine, sesame oil, and ginger juice. To combine and give the paste a smooth texture, stir it vigorously with a chopstick or fork, in one direction only, for several minutes.

Batter:
1/2 cup self-raising flour OR
1/2 cup all-purpose flour sifted with 1/4 teaspoon baking powder
1 tsp cornstarch

Add water to these ingredients and beat in order to make a batter of the consistency of heavy cream.

Eggplants:

If possible, use the narrowly cylindrical Asian variety. Peel them in longitudinal strips, creating stripes. Slice diagonally; make slices 1/2 inch apart; alternate one slice 3/4 through (making a slit for the stuffing) with one slice all the way through (making pieces).

Having prepared all of the above items, next stuff the eggplant pieces. Dust both surfaces of the slit in each piece with cornstarch and spread filling in the crevice. When all have been stuffed, dip them in batter and deep-fry. Drain on paper towels. Serve immediately with saucers of vinegar for dipping.

If you have more eggplant than filling—or, alternatively, no filling at all—simply dip eggplant slices alone in batter and deep-fry. Again, serve with vinegar dip and/or chilli sauce.

SZECHUAN QUICK BRAISED EGGPLANT

Eggplant
(Minced pork OR pressed bean curd)
Garlic
Ginger
Soy sauce (preferably a mixture of light and dark)
Chilli sauce (preferably the Shanghai broad bean chilli sauce known as *dau baan laat jeung*
Spring onions
Vinegar
Sesame oil

Chop the eggplant into strips, 2–3" long and 1/2" wide. Toss with salt and leave to drain 20–30 minutes; blot dry. Chop the spring onions into 1" lengths.

With hot oil in the wok, fry the pork or bean curd over high heat until cooked, then remove. Again heat the wok with oil; fry a crushed clove of garlic together with a crushed slice of ginger; add the eggplant; toss until the eggplant is quite limp. Return the meat or bean curd; season with soy sauce and chilli; cover and braise intensely for a minute or two. Uncover, add the spring onions, season with a splash of vinegar and a dash of sesame oil; toss yet again, then serve.

GREEN PAPAYA   *Mook gwa* 木瓜

APPEARANCE: Papayas eaten as a vegetable look like papayas eaten as fruit—except that their skin is green, or half-green half-yellow, and the flesh is white. All papayas have a smooth, almost waxy skin, and a generally elongated shape, which starts broad near the stem, narrows a bit in the middle, then bellows out before tapering to a blunt point. They all also have a central cavity, which in unripe fruits has white seeds (or none), and in ripe fruits has black seeds.

Three sorts of papaya reach the Hong Kong markets. The two imported varieties are sold as fruit and eaten only ripe, e.g. small (6-inch) 'Solo' papayas, and long (8–12-inch) narrow Thai papayas. The third, local variety (illustrated) is sold at fruit stands when ripe and in the vegetable markets when not. It is usually 6–12 inches long but broader (4–6 inches in diameter) than Thai fruits.

QUALITY: Select solid, firm, unblemished fruits. Half-ripe fruits are preferred for Chinese soups, while absolutely green fruits are preferred for Thai salads.

COMMENTS: Ripe papaya is soft, finely textured, and sweet—relentlessly delicate in flavor and texture, suitable only for serving as fresh fruit. Unripe, or green, papaya is hard, finely textured, and without definitive taste; eminently suitable for grating and braising or boiling. Half-ripe—not surprisingly—falls somewhere in the middle on all counts.

Nutritionists of both East and West agree that papaya is good for the stomach and the digestion. The source of its virtues seem to be a family of chemicals, of which papain is pre-eminent. This is a protein-digesting enzyme that occurs naturally in the latex of both leaves and fruit (particularly unripe fruit)—and that has been isolated, extracted, and sold separately as a digestive aid. Other chemicals are reputed to kill intestinal worms and to rejuvenate gastrointestinal membranes.

In spite of these virtues, in the green fruits the latex is a bit bitter and the texture a bit dense. Hence, they are usually combined with an ingredient to stimulate digestion (overcoming density), such as ginger or vinegar, and an ingredient to harmonize the bitterness, such as red dates, warming herbs, or a pinch of sugar.

COOKING:

Western Green papaya resembles summer melons in its cooking potential. Like cucumber it can be eaten raw; like summer squash it can be braised in casseroles or stir-fried. For these purposes it is best shredded or chopped finely because of its tough texture; green papaya with garlic, tomatoes, and oregano is a particularly complementary and tasty combination.

Last but not least, like winter squash it can be baked with a stuffing of seasoned meat or veg.

Chinese The Cantonese consider unripe papaya soup material. They prefer them half-ripe, and use them for both sweet and savory concoctions.

SAVORY PAPAYA SOUP
Green or half-ripe papaya, peeled and chopped
Fresh ginger, a thick slice, crushed
Red dates, rinsed and seeded
Either: Pork, lean meat or ribs, OR
   Tail of a grass carp, OR
   Peanuts (raw)

If using fish, scale, rinse, dry, rub with (coarse) salt, then fry quickly over fairly high heat until skin is golden on both sides. If using peanuts rinse them quickly in hot water. Combine papaya, ginger, dates, and fish or meat or peanuts in a large pot. Add 3–4 times as much water. Bring to the boil, simmer at least one hour (longer for the pork bones) until broth is reduced by 1/3–1/2. Season with salt, and serve.

DOUBLE-BOILED SWEET PAPAYA SOUP
Half-ripe papaya, peeled and chopped
Ginger, a small slice, crushed
(Silver wood's ear mushroom, *ngun yee* 銀耳)
(Red dates, *hoeng jo* 紅棗 , rinsed and seeded)
Rock sugar (*bing tong* 冰糖)

If using mushroom, soak it, preferably for several hours; clean it of any dark debris. Crush the sugar to bits by placing it in a cloth or plastic bag and hitting with a hammer or rolling pin. Place all ingredients in top pan of a double boiler over simmering water; cook 1–2 hours. The papaya will gradually generate its own broth. When the chunks have softened to the point of disintegration, serve the soup.

Chinese home-style double boilers are fashioned by placing a heatproof pot or casserole on top of a dish or trivet inside a larger pot of boiling water. The lid of the inner pot must extend beyond the rim of the pot itself to prevent water from leaking inside. The boiling water should reach about halfway up the side of the inner pot and must be replenished periodically. This process is called *dun*. It is not strictly necessary—one can simply boil the soup ingredients in water—but it does extract and preserve delicate flavors otherwise driven off by high temperature.

CHESTNUTS *Lut jee* 栗子

APPEARANCE: Appropriate to their northern origins, these nuts have two coats: an outer, hard, smooth shell; and an inner, furry, beige membrane which closely covers the convoluted yellow nutmeat. In markets, vendors generally have nuts in all stages of dress: some fully clothed (unshelled); some in just their underwear; and some naked.

QUALITY: Buying whole chestnuts can be exasperating because the inscrutable outer shell often hides unexpected mysteries of rot and decay. Select those that are firm, full (i.e. not dried with the nut rattling inside), and unblemished. The inner nut should be uniformly yellow and slightly resilient. Buying peeled nuts is safer but, of course, more expensive.

COMMENTS: Chestnuts are a northern temperate crop, familiar to Asians, Europeans, and North Americans alike. Each continent has its own species, although all apparently belong to the same genus. Thus appearances, tastes, and textures differ but only slightly.

Although edible raw, these nuts are usually cooked, either roasted, baked, boiled, or braised. The taste is sweet, the texture dense to the point of being pasty.

The Cantonese believe chestnuts are good for the kidneys, which in turn influence the immune system, longevity, and sexual prowess. Chinese doctors concur, elaborating that their warming nature increases energy throughout the body, and tonifies three of the major internal organs (spleen, stomach, and kidneys). Hence they are most appropriately served in winter, and most commonly prepared with chicken, which has the complementary effects of tonifying the liver and blood.

Dried chestnuts are also available in Chinese groceries. The older they are, the tougher and less flavorful; but this will not be obvious from the package. Soak them at least four hours (or overnight) before using, and expect them to require longer cooking than fresh.

PREPARATION: For roasting or baking, leave unshelled. For boiling or braising, remove outer shell with a knife and, in some fashion, remove the furry inner skin. Soaking them in hot water 2–3 minutes usually loosens the skins enough for easy peeling.

COOKING:

Western In the West, chestnuts are a winter delicacy, served in both sweet and savory forms—from English chestnut stuffing for the Christmas goose to the French *marrons glacés* to simple roasted chestnuts.

In other words, roast or boil whole chestnuts and eat out of hand. Or shell them, boil until soft, mash, and then use with savory ingredients to stuff poultry or with sweet rich ingredients to make cakes, mousses, and other desserts.

Chinese Most chestnuts imported into Hong Kong are consumed from small bags purchased from street vendors who roast them in mounds of charcoal. At home, cooks braise them with chicken, serve them in sauce over cabbage, or boil them in soups, both sweet and savory.

CHICKEN BRAISED WITH CHESTNUTS

Chicken pieces*
Chinese chestnuts: if fresh, shelled and peeled; if dried, soaked
Winter mushrooms, soaked
Spring onions, lower white portions only (or leek)
Ginger
Light and dark soy sauces

In a braising pot, in a little oil, brown chicken lightly. Add mushrooms; when fragrant, add chestnuts. When they too are lightly coated in oil, add spring onions and a few crushed pieces of ginger. Finally season with equal amounts of light and dark soy sauces, and add water to about one-half the depth of the ingredients. Simmer until chestnuts are tender and liquid is reduced, about 1 hour. Periodically check, stir, and add more water if the casserole has cooked dry. When ready to serve, adjust seasoning with soy sauce and thickness of sauce with cornstarch if required; serve.

*Instead of real chicken, you may substitute chunks of gluten or the soy-based vegetarian chicken known as *jai gai*.

WAN DING BO

12 chestnuts, shelled and peeled
1/2 cup pearl barley (*yeung yee mai* 洋薏米)
1 sheet dried bean curd skin (*foo jook* 腐竹)
6 quail eggs (*aam chun daan* 鵪鶉蛋) or 3 hen's eggs; hard-boiled and shelled
Sugar to taste

Combine chestnuts and barley in 6 cups of water; bring to the boil. Crumble the bean curd skin into bits as small as possible. When the water reaches a rolling boil, add the bean curd skin bits slowly as the water froths. Continue to simmer until chestnuts are tender, the barley has swollen, and the bean curd has mostly dissolved into a white broth. Sweeten to taste, add eggs, and when heated through, serve.

CALTROPS *Ling gok* 菱角

APPEARANCE: The bizarre shape of these nuts leaves no room for misidentification. They measure about 2 inches from tip to tip, with a smooth shell as hard as the horns they resemble. The inner nutmeat—as they are sometimes sold shelled—is also wing-tipped but creamy-white in color, as illustrated.

QUALITY: Unshelled nuts are difficult to evaluate. Choose those that look sound and smell fresh. When cracked, the meat should fill the inner cavity and be uniformly white.

COMMENTS: Three species of the genus *Trapa* have been providing human food since neolithic times. *T. bicornuta,* the species illustrated here, was an important staple in parts of China before the 20th century. *T. bispinosa,* the Singhara nut, also with two horns, is eaten by the people of Kashmir; while *T. natans,* the Jesuit's nut, with four horns, is reported to have been a common food of ancient Europeans.

Ling gok resemble potatoes in three respects. First, in color both are white. Second, in flavor both are bland, predominantly starchy foods. Third, in texture they are crunchy when raw and somewhat mealy when cooked.

In addition to consumption as food, whole unshelled nuts are dried—simply left at room temperature—for use as lucky talismans. They can sometimes be spotted decoratively strung on silk cords and hung, for example, from the rearview mirrors inside automobiles.

Caltrops in the shell, refrigerated, will keep several weeks. Shelled nuts must be eaten within two days of purchase because they quickly decay. Check each nutmeat carefully for soft spots before using.

PREPARATION: With a sturdy knife and sharp blows, cut off the horns where they begin to flare to meet the body of the nut. To eat them raw, peel off the rest in any way you can (in Wuhan, people use their teeth). To cook them, simply put in water, bring to the boil, simmer 5–10 minutes until done; then peel.

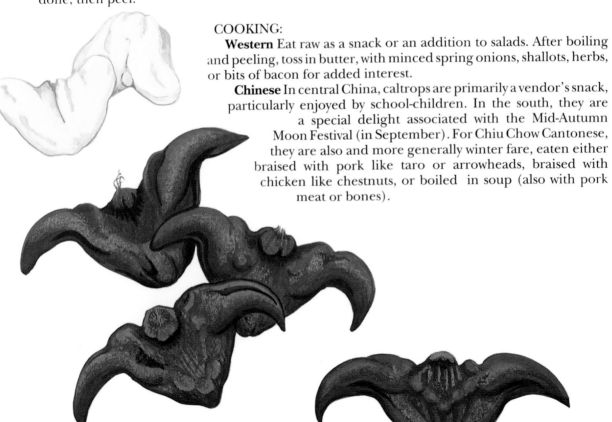

COOKING:

Western Eat raw as a snack or an addition to salads. After boiling and peeling, toss in butter, with minced spring onions, shallots, herbs, or bits of bacon for added interest.

Chinese In central China, caltrops are primarily a vendor's snack, particularly enjoyed by school-children. In the south, they are a special delight associated with the Mid-Autumn Moon Festival (in September). For Chiu Chow Cantonese, they are also and more generally winter fare, eaten either braised with pork like taro or arrowheads, braised with chicken like chestnuts, or boiled in soup (also with pork meat or bones).

NIGHT-FRAGRANT FLOWER   *Yeh heung fa* 夜香花

APPEARANCE: Each piece is an inflorescence, or cluster of flower buds, about 2 inches long, more or less green. Usually several of the buds will have bloomed into bright yellow five-petalled flowers, further confirming the identification.

QUALITY: Select those with more buds and fewer flowers.

COMMENTS: The plant that produces this rather precious vegetable is a woody climber of the butterfly weed or milkweed family. A native of China and India, it is cultivated in Europe as an ornamental and in the Asian tropics and subtropics as a source of food: flowers and leaves are eaten as a vegetable, while a sweetmeat is made from the fleshy roots.
   The flowers are undoubtedly rich in vitamins and minerals due to the nature of the petals, pollen, and incipient seeds and fruit present. The flavor is mild and pleasant; the texture—when only lightly cooked, as they should be—resembles very tender peapods.

PREPARATION: Rinse quickly and shake dry.

COOKING: An uncommon vegetable, the Cantonese seem content to serve this in only two ways: stir-fried with egg, or in soup. For the egg dish, simply wilt the flowers in a little oil, then add beaten, seasoned egg, and cook to desired degree of firmness. Soup with *yeh heung fa* usually involves pork liver. For this, slice and season the liver with ginger juice, salt, and pepper. Bring water to the boil, add the vegetable and liver, simmer only briefly until both are just done, and serve immediately.

STEM LETTUCE *Woh sun* 萵苣

APPEARANCE: At first sight identify this vegetable by its stem: 10–15 inches long, 1–2 inches in diameter, covered with prominent reddish (leaf) scars and topped with a cluster of leaves. Note that the leaves lack stalks and have the light green color and thin texture of ordinary leaf lettuce.

QUALITY: Choose those with stems of large diameter and white, firm pith. Look for and avoid those with signs of wet rot, especially on the leaf scars or at the center of the base.

COMMENTS: Stem lettuce has been grown for centuries in northern China, where the leaves are cooked fresh and the stem is pickled. This explains why Chinese canned 'pickled lettuce' unexpectedly resembles a root more than a leaf. An American seed company introduced this vegetable to the West in 1942 under the name 'celtuce'.

The choicest part of this vegetable is the heart of the stem, which has the faint flavor of lettuce and the juicy, crunchy texture of tender celery (hence the name, cel-tuce). Like other lettuces, it is considered a 'cooling' vegetable with a bitter-sweet flavor that can improve the function of the stomach. Eating it raw accentuates these properties, whereas cooking it, especially with oil and ginger or garlic, tends to harmonize them.

PREPARATION: Remove leaves, wash, drain, and use separately. Rinse the stem; peel off the sheath of tough outer fibres. Chop the pith as desired.

COOKING:
Western Toss the leaves in salad. Eat the stem as is; or chop and toss in salad; or marinate with other vegetables in an Italian or oil and vinegar dressing.
Chinese The bulk of China's stem lettuce crop goes into pickles. You may attempt something similar by marinating parboiled bits of stem in soy sauce and oil.

Stem lettuce that is used fresh is generally cut in matchsticks and stir-fried randomly with pork, poultry, and/or other vegetables. Stem lettuce with peas or sugar peapods, spring onions, and chicken, is a particularly flavorful combination.

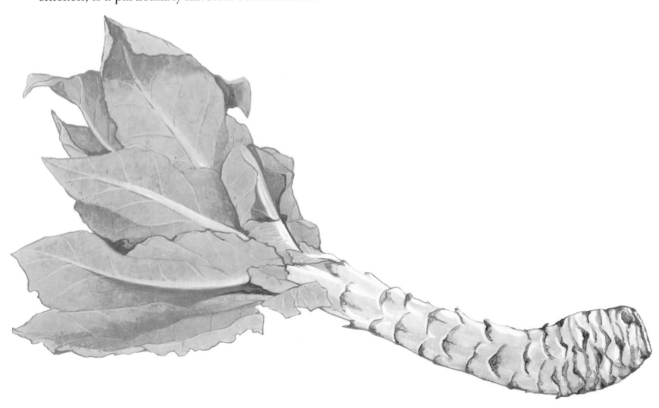

CELERY *Kun choi* 芹菜

APPEARANCE: Asian celery looks just like its Western supermarket counterpart, except it is more lean, green, and leafy. Stalks seldom measure more than 1/2 inch in diameter, and entire bunches seldom more than 2 inches, even at the base.

QUALITY: Select plants with the fattest and whitest (i.e. most tender) stalks. Check for worm holes in cracks in the stalks.

COMMENTS: Apparently both Euro-American and Chinese celeries represent a single species that has diverged in development over the past 1,500 years. Both have the same aromatic flavor, crunchy-crisp texture, and stringy nature; the Chinese type is simply stronger on all counts. It is also more nutritious, having more of virtually everything in the way of vitamins and (particularly) minerals than its milder cousin.

In terms of Chinese nutrition, celery is considered to be neutral (neither hot nor cold, wet nor dry) but powerful in its calming effect on the liver. Hence it is a home tonic for lowering blood pressure and cholesterol, and a natural choice for cooking with high cholesterol foods, particularly seafood.

Celery is something of a lucky charm as well. The Cantonese traditionally include their celery in vegetarian dishes served during the Chinese Lunar New Year. Eating *kun choi* on the first day of the year bestows *kun lik* (i.e. diligence, and the strength to work hard) throughout the coming year. Furthermore, eating it with the black hair seaweed *faat choi* (髮菜) ensures that this diligence will bring ever increasing (i.e. *faat* 發) wealth (i.e. *choi* 財).

PREPARATION: Separate leaf stalks and wash well. Remove the string-like fibres in the ribs. Chop as desired, preferably in matchsticks or long diagonals for Chinese stir-frying.

COOKING:

Western While the larger but milder Western celery can be eaten raw or cooked, as seasoning or as vegetable, the toughness and strong flavor of the Chinese variety restrict it to cooking and flavoring purposes. Use it for soup stocks, casseroles, and vegetable medleys such that it tantalizes but does not overwhelm.

Chinese Hong Kong Cantonese actually cook *sai kun*, or foreign celery, more often than their own, presumably because the former is milder, more tender, and—possibly now—more widely available. Nevertheless, either variety can be stir-fried with other meats (particularly kidneys), poultry, vegetables (particularly mung bean sprouts), or seafood (particularly squid).

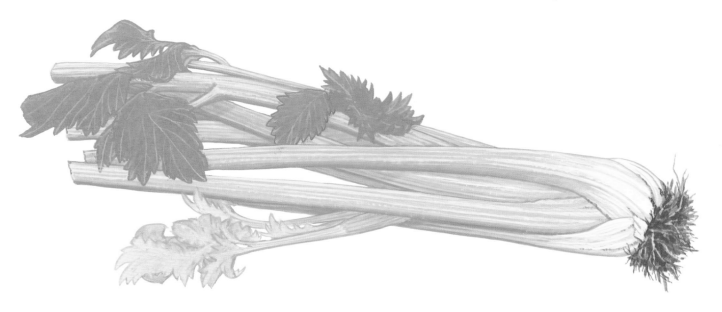

NEW YEAR'S PROSPERITY DISH
1 cup Chinese celery, chopped in 1-inch lengths
1/4 cup dried seahair (*faat choi* 髮菜)
10 deep-fried gluten puffs (*saang gun* 生筋)
1 slice fresh ginger, crushed
1 tbsp oyster sauce

Rehydrate seaweed by covering in water for 30 minutes or more; drain. Then rinse with hot water, drain, and rub with a teaspoon or so of oil, separating the strands so that they will not cling together in a single clump during cooking.

Parboil the gluten puffs to remove dirt and excess oil; drain.

To cook, heat oil in wok and season with ginger; when oil is very hot, add celery. Stir and toss until fragrant and just beginning to look cooked, then add seaweed and wheat puffs. Season with oyster sauce, add 1/2 cup water or light stock, cover and simmer strongly 3–4 minutes. Adjust seasoning. Sauce should be thick; if not, remove vegetables and quickly boil it down or thicken with cornstarch, pour the sauce over and serve.

CELERY & SQUID
Equal quantities of squid or cuttlefish, and of celery
Cooking wine or sherry
(Sesame oil)

To prepare squid/cuttlefish, remove head with tendrils; discard head but save tendrils. Strip purplish skin from body and remove its single white, plate-like bone. Lay the body on the cutting board, skin side up. With sharp knife score it in a grid pattern; finally cut it into rectangles approximately 1 x 1/2 inch in size.

Chop celery in long, thin diagonal pieces.

To cook the dish, with hot oil in wok stir-fry celery until fragrant and remove. Add more oil; add squid; toss until pieces curl and turn white. Sprinkle with wine or sherry, season with salt, white pepper, a dash of vinegar, and a pinch of sugar. Return celery. Toss and simmer furiously to blend flavors. If liquid has accumulated, thicken with cornstarch. Finally, you may add a drop or two of sesame oil to give the dish richness, aroma, and sheen; serve.

WILD RICE SHOOTS   *Gau sun* 膠筍

APPEARANCE: The shoot in the illustration has been cut in half to show its inner pith. As sold in the market, whole shoots are 10–15 inches long, and taper from about 1 inch in diameter at the base to a point at the leafy tip.

QUALITY: Select firm, fresh shoots with broad, white bases. Since only the solid pith of the stem is eaten, the greater its diameter the greater the proportion of food per stalk. Young shoots will be lily-white in cross section; older shoots develop black pin-dots (as illustrated below), which indicate that both flavor and texture have begun to decline.

COMMENTS: This plant apparently belongs to the same species that North American Indians traditionally cultivated for grain, which is now known as 'wild rice'—and which is of a different genus altogether from ordinary rice. Wild rice occurs through the middle of Asia, from Japan to Indo-China, but is consistently cultivated there as a vegetable rather than as a grain crop. To be absolutely accurate, it is not the rice shoot that is cultivated and consumed: it is a fungus that invades the shoots, causing them to swell—and eventually causing the black dots (spores) to appear in the center of the stalks.

The texture of wild rice shoots could be described as a cross between two other white vegetables, potatoes and eggplant. Firm yet moist, they have little inherent flavor but readily absorb and enhance companion flavors. A botanist travelling in China in the early 20th century, perhaps tiring of exotic Asian delicacies, asserted, 'From a European standpoint [*gau sun*] is really very good eating.'

Nutritionally, like other fungi, *gau sun* is classified as somewhat 'cooling' in effect and sweet in flavor. As with bamboo shoots, the Cantonese are wary of it, believing it to be somewhat poisonous and recommending those who feel weak to avoid it.

PREPARATION: Peel off and discard all leaves. Slice inner shoot in long diagonals for stir-frying, or otherwise as desired.

COOKING:

Western Sauté; bake; steam and serve buttered or sauced. The mild flavor and spongy texture invites seasoning with herbs or combining with intensely flavored ingredients such as bacon, ham or anchovies.

Chinese As with other less common vegetables, Hong Kong Cantonese serve this one simply: inevitably stir-fried, usually with shreds of beef or pork.

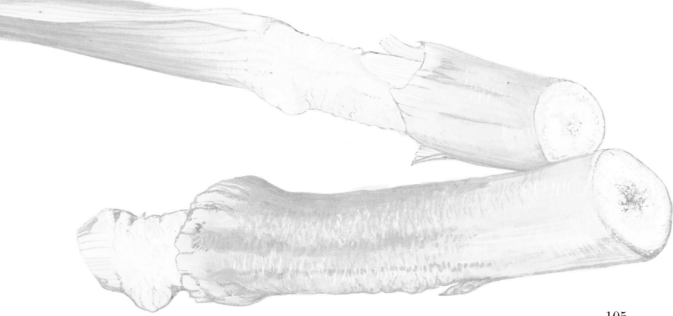

BAMBOO SHOOTS *Sun* 筍

APPEARANCE: Every bamboo produces shoots, but only 10–15 of the hundred or so species produce shoots that reach markets. These fall into three broad categories:

Spring bamboo shoots or *mo sun* 毛筍 , as illustrated below, measure an impressive 3–5 inches in diameter at the base and 10 inches or so in length; the outer leaves are fuzzy, hence the Chinese name, which translates as 'hair shoots'.

Winter bamboo shoots or *doeng sun* 冬筍 , are about half the size but identical in shape to spring shoots; these are dug up while the shoot is still dormant or just beginning to grow.

Summer bamboo shoots or *jook sun* 竹筍 , a small species that produces shoots the size of thin asparagus, seldom available in markets outside of China.

QUALITY: Each species of bamboo shoot has its characteristic flavor and degree of sweetness, as well as size and season. Nevertheless, certain generalities hold true: winter shoots are the choicest; smaller shoots of any variety are more tender; those less green should be sweeter.

COMMENTS: This vegetable is most appreciated in northern China where it commonly and regularly appears in a great range of dishes. In some cookbooks from those regions, entire sections are devoted to this single vegetable and writers gush, '[Bamboo shoots] are considered one of the best Chinese vegetables, preferable to meat in terms of texture, nutrients, and flavor.'

Conversely, if not perversely, the Cantonese consume this vegetable warily. They consider it marginally poisonous, hard to digest, and potentially damaging to anyone with a skin wound.

Taking a more dispassionate view, Chinese nutritionists agree with both sides that bamboo shoots are powerful, and attribute the different opinions to different climates and cooking styles. Bamboo shoots' 'cold' energy is exceptionally suited to harmonize the warm or hot energy of meat. Hence, they are appropriate for northern cuisines, in which long-cooking methods and meats predominate, while less so for the warmer climate of Canton, where less meat and lighter cooking styles prevail.

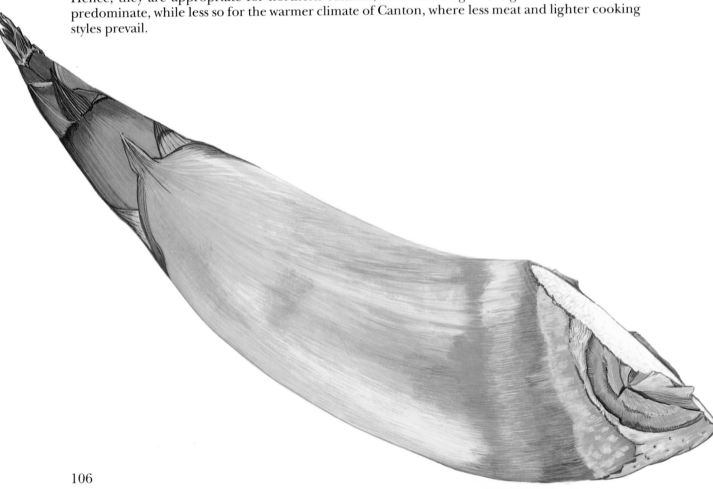

PREPARATION: Fresh bamboo shoots contain a bitter poison, hydrocyanic acid, which must be eliminated before they are eaten. Parboiling is the accepted method of handling this problem. To prepare bamboo shoots for cooking, first strip off all leaves. Then, using a sharp, thin knife, slice off and discard the tough base. The central core is the edible part; you may parboil it whole or sliced. Put into cold water, bring to the boil, simmer—4–5 minutes for slices, 20 minutes for the whole shoot—drain, rinse, and sample. If the shoots still taste bitter, boil again; otherwise proceed.

Refrigerated, unpeeled bamboo shoots can keep for weeks. You can peel, slice, and parboil the end gradually as needed; or you can prepare the whole shoot at once and refrigerate or freeze unused pieces for later use.

Canned bamboo shoots may be used straight from the can.

COOKING:

Western After parboiling, bamboo shoots may be served immediately as a side dish; they may be further sautéed, baked, or braised with other vegetables; or marinated; or chilled for later addition to tossed salads. Following the Chinese example, cook them with mushrooms and serve them with meat.

Chinese As mentioned above, bamboo shoots figure prominently in the cuisines of Peking and Shanghai. They appear in soups, casseroles, dumplings, noodle dishes, and meat and vegetable combinations, in homes and restaurants. They go well with meat, and are considered particularly compatible with winter mushrooms.

More generally, then, bamboo shoots can be used to advantage in virtually any vegetable and meat stir-fry or casserole. Shredded pork and bamboo shoots is a popular dish; diced pork with bamboo shoots and green peppers in sauce made with chillies, garlic, and black beans is even more so.

In vegetable dishes with bamboo shoots but without meat, using more oil, rich companions (e.g. gluten, deep-fried bean curd) and longer cooking times will help balance their naturally 'cold' nature. Deep-fried bamboo shoots stir-fried with salted mustard greens is a simple example; the following is more elaborate.

BRAISED BAMBOO SHOOTS & MUSHROOMS
Bamboo shoots, parboiled
Winter mushrooms, soaked
Baak choi, parboiled

Use approximately equal parts bamboo shoots and mushrooms. Slice bamboo shoots in 1/8-inch-thick, bite-sized rectangles. Squeeze the mushrooms dry (saving the liquid for braising later). For the best flavor, briefly deep-fry bamboo shoots and mushrooms. In a small amount of oil, then fry a piece of ginger until fragrant; add mushrooms and shoots. Toss while sprinkling with a little wine; when the sizzling dies away, season with soy sauce and a dash of sugar. Add stock (with mushroom soaking liquid); cover and simmer vigorously until liquid reduces; thicken with cornstarch if needed, then pour over the cooked cabbage on a serving plate.

STRAW MUSHROOMS   *Cho gwu* 草菇

APPEARANCE: These are about 1 inch tall and wide. When young and fresh, they are beige and firm. With age, they darken, become slightly slimy, and fracture, as the umbrella-like mushroom cap grows through its surrounding membrane.

QUALITY: Select the youngest, i.e. those that are pale, small, firm, and whole.

COMMENTS: The name of this mushroom derives from the fact that it was originally cultivated on rice-straw; modern farmers have discovered it does equally well on fertilized cotton wool—but the old name sticks. *Cho gwu* are comparable to the field or button mushroom of the West in mild taste, firm cooking texture, and ease of mass production.

All mushrooms are remarkably high in B vitamins, with above average amounts of protein, phosphorus, and potassium. Straw mushrooms are no exception. Chinese nutritionists consider them to have 'cool' energy, and the ability to reduce blood fat. Hence they go well with virtually any flesh or fowl, and combine particularly well with other vegetables, notoriously low in the Bs.

These mushrooms are difficult to store. Whether in the fridge or out, in a plastic bag or ventilated basket, they soon begin to deteriorate. Plan to use them within two days of purchase.

Dried straw mushrooms are also available. Rehydrated, they have as much, if not more, flavor than the fresh and a more chewy texture.

PREPARATION: Wash well, especially the lower ends, which generally need trimming. Peeling is unnecessary. For the best flavor, parboil whole mushrooms a minute or two before further cooking in order to remove a raw, earthy—almost moldy—component of their flavor. (Rehydrated dried mushrooms do not need parboiling.)

COOKING:
Western Straw mushrooms can substitute for Western button mushrooms in virtually any recipe except those that require a cap—e.g. stuffed mushrooms. Slice these, or leave the small ones whole. Sauté in butter, possible with herbs or spices; combine with meats and other vegetables in casseroles; or use as the foundation for cream of mushroom soups and sauces.

Chinese These are the only mushrooms that the Cantonese commonly eat fresh. Generally, they are served whole, either braised or boiled. (Beware that this is easier said than done because using chopsticks to retrieve sauce-coated *cho gwu* from a platter requires considerable manual dexterity.) Generally, too, straw mushrooms are cooked with other delicately flavored ingredients, such as fish, shellfish, bean curd, and lettuce, although they go equally well with the rich taste of a black bean sauce. They are popular in vegetarian dishes, in soups, congee, casseroles, and stir-fried mixtures.

MUSHROOMS IN BLACK BEAN SAUCE

Either: 1 lb pork ribs, chopped in 1–2 inch lengths, seasoned OR
        bean curd, fresh or deep-fried
1/2 lb straw mushrooms
3–4 cloves garlic, crushed
1–2 tsp fermented black beans
(Chilli, fresh, powder, paste, or sauce)

Mash garlic and beans together. In hot oil in wok, fry this paste until fragrant; if using pork or bean curd, add it now. Toss until browned; add a pinch of sugar, dashes of light and dark soy sauce, (chilli) and water to a depth of about 1/4 of the ingredients; simmer until cooked. Add mushrooms; simmer another 3–4 minutes until mushrooms are cooked as well. Adjust seasoning; if sauce seems too thin, thicken it with cornstarch; serve.

BRAISED MUSHROOMS & CRAB

2 cups straw mushrooms
1 cup crab meat, flaked finely
1 1/2 cups light stock, or water and a chicken stock cube
Green leafy vegetable, e.g. lettuce, pea tendrils, or one of the Chinese cabbages

Stir-fry green vegetable and arrange on a serving dish.
In wok or saucepan, simmer mushrooms in stock. When cooked, add crab meat with dashes of wine and white pepper to taste; continue to simmer until flavors are thoroughly blended. Thicken sauce with 1 tablespoon cornstarch mixed to a paste with a little water. Adjust seasoning with salt. At the last moment, stir in a teaspoon of oil (preferably sesame), to give the dish fragrance and shine, and pour over the green vegetable.

LOTUS ROOT *Leen ngau* 蓮藕

APPEARANCE: This vegetable looks like stiff strings of fat sausages. The sections measure 2–3 inches in diameter, come in two lengths (short, 3–4 inches; and long, 6–10 inches), and are separated from each other by narrow 'necks' whence leaf shoots emerge. They are quite hard, usually encrusted with pond mud, and—when seen in cross section—full of holes.

QUALITY: Examine lotus roots carefully, despite the mud, searching for soft spots and/or any sort of perforations in the skin. Soft spots suggest decay while perforations allow the mud inside; both conditions render the root virtually inedible. The sections elongate with age; hence the short sections are younger and usually more tender.

COMMENTS: The lotus is an ancient, multi-purpose Asian plant that supplies a host of edible products. Dried leaves are used as fragrant wrappers for rice dumplings; entire seedpods are boiled in medicinal soups; seeds are used whole in sweet and savory tonics, or puréed to make lotus seed paste for stuffing mooncakes and other confections.

The root is highly respected as a vegetable, appearing in many forms (i.e. fresh, dried, powdered), in many dishes, in many parts of China. Its flavor is mildly sweet, its texture crunchy, and its appearance exotic. In cross section, the canals of the bulb (properly termed 'rhizome', a subterranean stem) create an enchanting if not appetizing pattern.

According to Chinese nutritional theory, lotus is as exceptional in its effects on the body as it is in its appearance. It is considered to have a sweet flavor and neutral energy, with the ability to tonify three of the major internal organ-circuits. Being fundamentally neutral, its nature changes with cooking, and it needs no supporting ingredients to harmonize its properties. Raw lotus is said to cool the blood and clear heat. After an hour or two of cooking, it becomes nourishing and is said to build blood and stimulate appetite.

PREPARATION: Wash well. The surface has a thin skin, which is best removed by scraping with the upper, square edge of a wooden chopstick or the blunt edge of a knife blade. This process leaves the root shiny and beige—but vulnerable to discoloration when exposed to air. Hence, work quickly and/or immerse it in water as you go.

When cutting, discard the necks between the bulbs. The rest can be: shredded; carefully sliced for decorative pieces; or ruthlessly crushed and chopped. The last method is particularly recommended for soup, i.e. lay the whole bulb on the chopping board, smash with the broad side of a cleaver, then chop in 2-inch lengths, tearing the pieces apart lengthwise into bite-sized bits.

COOKING:

Western Like other starchy vegetables, lotus root may be boiled, braised, sautéed or deep-fried. It retains its crunchy texture even after hours of cooking, and hence is appropriate for crockpot casseroles. It can also be eaten raw, or parboiled and lightly pickled for consumption in or as salad.

Chinese Lotus root is used for sweet and savory dishes, both the mundane and the festive. During the Lunar New Year season, slices of lotus root (among other root vegetables, including carrot and winter melon) are candied and served as snacks. At other special times, whole roots are stuffed with glutinous rice and braised in sugar syrup.

On the savory side, lotus root may be stir-fried, braised, or boiled, generally with fatter cuts of meat or poultry. For stir-frying, shred the cleaned root with a potato peeler, rinse in cold water, then stir-fry as usual. Braised dishes take two forms. Either the root is chopped or it is left whole. In the former case, the addition of pork, peanuts, red dates, and soy sticks is common (see below). The latter case is usually a festive dish, in which the root is stuffed with mung beans and braised with duck.

Soup with lotus is also common. Companion ingredients are typically: peanuts and red dates (as with the braised dish); oysters, black-eyed peas (*mei dau* 眉豆), and seahair (*faat choi* 髮菜); or pork and squid, as described below.

BRAISED LOTUS

Pork: either meat, spare ribs, or trotter; OR
     Soy beans, soaked at least one hour; OR
     Soy milk sticks (*jee jook* 枝竹), soaked
Lotus root, peeled and chopped or sliced
Fermented red bean curd cheese (*naam yu* 南乳)*, 1/4–1/2 square per 6 inches or so of lotus
(Peanuts, raw, about 2 tbsp per 6 inches of root)
Sugar, or red dates (*hoeng jo* 紅棗)
Soy sauce

In a braising pot, brown pork (or soy beans or sticks) and lotus. Add bean curd cheese, peanuts (if desired), and a small amount of water; stir, making a special effort to disperse the cheese into a sauce. Add water to a depth of about 1/2 inch, season with soy sauce and a hefty pinch of sugar (or red dates). Simmer this concoction, covered, on low heat until lotus and meat are tender, 1–2 hours. Stir occasionally and add water as necessary to prevent sticking or burning. Adjust seasoning with soy sauce, and serve.

Well-cooked and ladled into clean containers, this dish will keep for at least a week in the fridge.

*A combination of equal parts dark and light soy sauces may be substituted for the *naam yu*. The taste will differ, and the sauce will not thicken—add a cornstarch paste if you want more of a gravy.

OCTO-PORK SOUP

1 small dried octopus (*jeung yu* 鱆魚)
1/2 lb pork bones
6–10 inches lotus root, peeled and chopped
Small hunk of fresh ginger, peeled, crushed

The octopus will measure 5–6 inches long and will be held, stretched open, by a small stick of wood. Remove the wood; rinse the octopus. Combine all ingredients in a large pot with about twice as much water. Bring to the boil and simmer 2–4 hours until broth is well-flavored and reduced by 1/3–1/2. Season with salt and serve.

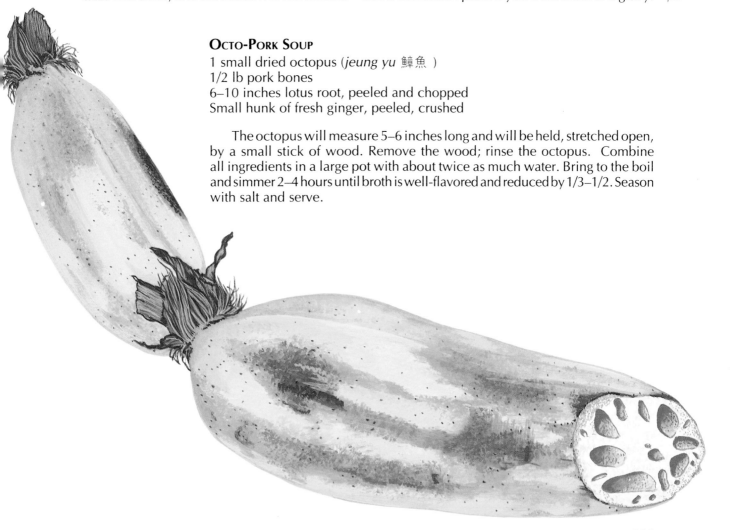

STEM GINGER *Jee geung* 子薑

APPEARANCE: It has the shape of ginger but the clear, moist skin of a new potato. Whole pieces are irregularly branched, with branches about 1/2 inch in diameter and encircled at 1-inch intervals by beige or pinkish lines. These lines recall where leaves were once attached—as they still are on the bright pink growing tips.

QUALITY: The older the 'hands', as they are called, the more fibrous; hence, select pieces with many young pink buds and smooth, clear yellowish skin.

COMMENTS: Stem ginger is the newest growth of the ginger rhizome (a rhizome being an underground stem). Old, mellowed ginger with its dry, brown skin is used as a seasoning (q.v.), but these young upstarts are eaten fresh as a vegetable or are pickled. They have a fresh, fragrant flavor that is more sweet than spicy, and a tender but crisp texture.

Stem ginger is considered to be identical in action but milder in strength, when compared with old 'cooking' ginger. Specifically, then, it has a warm, downward-moving energy that can settle the stomach. Being tender, it can be chewed raw or used in cooking as a vegetable.

PREPARATION: Scrape surface lightly using a small knife with its blade held perpendicular to the ginger's surface; rinse. For pickling, chop at the joints into chunks to fit your containers. For stir-frying, slice as thinly as possible across the grain with long diagonal cuts. In either case, salt it first. Place the bits in a large bowl, sprinkle with salt (preferably coarse) and toss to mix. Cantonese cooks maintain that the ginger will have a crisper texture, with less bruises, if tossed rather than mixed with a spoon or a hand. Grasp the sides of the bowl with both hands and flick your wrists to toss the bowl's contents lightly into the air.

COOKING:

Western For variety of texture and less pungent flavor, add minced stem ginger where the powdered spice is specified, e.g. spice cookies, gingerbread, fruitcakes, pumpkin pie, bread pudding. Sauté it with bland vegetables, such as courgettes. Or add pickled ginger to salads, particularly with yoghurt, cucumber, and water chestnuts.

Chinese The bulk of Canton's stem ginger crop probably ends up preserved in sugar and exported to the West in 'ginger jars' as a sweetmeat. Most Cantonese, however, withdraw in polite distaste from the very idea of sweet ginger and instead prefer to eat theirs pickled. Thin slices of

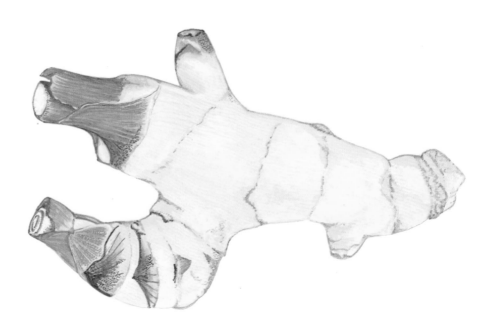

pickled ginger with black preserved duck egg (*pei daan*) is a common snack, an hors d'oeuvre , or a quick dinner dish to accompany rice. Stem ginger—either before or after pickling—may be stir-fried. The Cantonese traditionally combine it with beef (as described below) or chicken, but other possibilities are legion. Use it where sweet pungency can balance and accent other delicate flavors, as with mung bean sprouts or melon.

PICKLED GINGER

1 lb stem ginger
1 tsp salt (preferably coarse)
2 cups white vinegar
1 clove garlic, crushed
2 cups white granulated sugar

Wash, scrape, rinse, and salt ginger as described above. Toss it 5–6 times every 5 minutes for 20 minutes. The salt will draw juice from the ginger so that the finished pickles will be crisp. Meanwhile bring the vinegar to the boil; add a pinch of salt, the garlic, and the sugar. Simmer gently for 3–4 minutes until the sugar has dissolved and the garlic has yielded its flavor. Sample the brew and adjust its sweet-to-sour balance to your own taste.

When the ginger is ready, blot each piece dry. Place in hot jars and pour the hot pickling liquid over; all the ginger should be immersed (and should soon turn pink). When cool—and within 3 hours for best results—refrigerate.

The ginger will be ready to eat after 3 days, and will keep for at least a year in the fridge.

BEEF & STEM GINGER

1–2 inches of fresh or pickled stem ginger*
Approximately twice this volume of beef, sliced thinly across the grain and seasoned
Spring onions or flowering garlic chives (*gau choi fa* 韭菜花), chopped in 1-inch lengths

If using fresh stem ginger, prepare it for stir-frying as described under 'Preparation'. After tossing with salt, let the slices rest 5–10 minutes, then rinse well and blot dry.

To cook, heat oil in wok, add ginger, stir and toss for 2 minutes, add onions, season with salt, stir, and cook until shiny and fragrant; remove. Reheat wok with oil, sear beef quickly, return vegetables. Stir and toss to blend flavors, adding only a splash of water if necessary to prevent sticking; adjust seasoning with light soy sauce, and dish.

*If using pickled ginger, rinse well in water, blot dry, then slice in thin diagonal slices. To cook, sear beef, immediately add ginger and onions, continue to toss and cook until beef is done; adjust seasoning with soy sauce, and dish.

TARO *Wu tau* 芋頭

APPEARANCE: To distinguish this from other root vegetables, note that its brown, hairy skin has fine, dark rings that encircle it at regular intervals and thick roots that emerge at irregular intervals. When cut, the white flesh is flecked with purple.

All taros are heavy, dense objects of oval shape, but varying size. The two varieties commonly sold in Hong Kong—and representative of the two great divisions of taro varieties worldwide (see comments below)—are:

Betel-Nut Taro (*Bun long wu tau* 檳榔芋頭): large, up to 4 inches in diameter and a foot in length;

Red-Budded Taro (*Hoeng nga wu tau* 紅芽芋頭): small, 1–2 inches in diameter—i.e. of about the same size and shape as a large duck egg—and often with a pink shoot beginning to emerge from one end.

QUALITY: Scrutinize the skin to be sure tubers have no soft spots or worm holes. Buds, if present, should be small and bright pink.

COMMENTS: In the 2,000 years that Asians, Africans, and Polynesians have been cultivating taro, more than 200 varieties have been developed. All appear to belong to one species, in two main subgroups: the *dasheen* of Trinidad and the West Indies, which produces a large central tuber (like the betel-nut taro); and the *eddoe*, which produces many smaller tubers (like the red-budded taro).

In general, like potato, taro is a starchy tuber of bland taste. The many varieties differ in appearance as well as flavor and texture, but certain generalizations hold true. First, all parts contain calcium oxalate, which when raw can cause allergic reactions in some people, and which must be cooked to be eaten safely. Second, taro starch is exceptionally fine-grained; hence its texture is smoother and creamier than other roots, tubers, and grains.

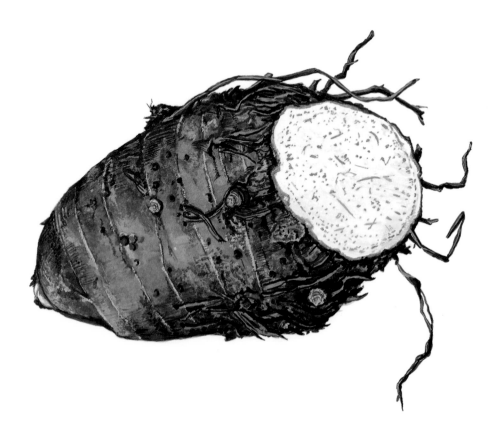

Despite its attractive texture and flavor, many Cantonese reckon taro is a vegetable 'to be careful of'. It is said to affect the stomach; in moderation, it helps digestion, but too much can cause indigestion, and each individual must find his own limits. In cooking it is invariably associated with oil—e.g. deep-fried (as shreds, mashed patties, etc) or cooked with duck (an oily bird) or coconut—which may both lubricate its path through the digestive system and discourage people from eating too much.

PREPARATION: Small taros may be left whole for baking or boiling. Larger ones must be peeled and chopped. Those who are sensitive to its allergenic chemicals should wear rubber gloves for this task, or recruit an assistant.

COOKING:

Western Taro substitutes admirably for potatoes in almost any recipe. It may be boiled, baked, braised, mashed, sautéed, deep-fried, or stewed. The smaller varieties are particularly tender and choice. As with new potatoes, they are perhaps best appreciated simply boiled and buttered. Or wrapped in foil and baked in the oven or in the coals of a barbecue pit. The larger taro is drier, more pasty and coarse in texture, so it benefits from long cooking or braising with slightly fatty cuts of meat.

Chinese The traditional Cantonese way of eating small red-budded taros is to boil them in their jackets, peel and eat them in the hand by the light of the Mid-Autumn Festival full moon. The large taros are used at Chinese New Year to make crisp snacks ('Taro Nests', described below). At other times and for other purposes, large and small varieties are interchangeable. Vegetarian restaurants serve deep-fried coin-sized croquettes with sweet and sour sauce; other restaurants serve it mashed, spread on thin slices of duck, and deep-fried; hotpot restaurants serve it braised in casserole with chicken and coconut milk.

At home, cooks serve the following:

BRAISED TARO WITH COCONUT

2–3 cups taro, peeled and chopped in chunks
1 large clove garlic, crushed
Grated or desiccated (but not sweetened) coconut or coconut milk
(Winter mushrooms)
(Duck or chicken)
Soy sauce (light or dark, or a little of both)

Heat oil in saucepan or casserole; sauté garlic (and any meat and/or mushrooms to be added), then add taro. Stir and cook until lightly browned. Season with soy sauce(s) or salt; add coconut, and finally 1/2–1 cup water (if you are not using coconut milk). Simmer until taro is tender—the length of time will depend on the taro, from 15 minutes to an hour. Adjust seasoning and serve.

STEAMED PORK & TARO

1 1/2 cups taro, peeled, coarsely grated
1/2 cup lean pork, minced, seasoned
Additional ingredients as desired:
    Winter mushrooms, soaked, chopped
    Dried shrimp, soaked, cleaned, minced

Combine all ingredients. Add approximately 1/4 cup hot water, season with salt, pepper, a tablespoon of oil, and 1/2–1 teaspoon cornstarch. Mix well. Place in a shallow dish or enamel pan; steam over boiling water or cooking rice until pork is cooked.

Savory Taro Pudding (Wu Tau Go 芋頭糕)

Follow the directions and recipe for *Loh Baak Go*, p 118, substituting small cubes of taro for the grated radish. This pudding is less common than the radish version, but is smoother in texture and more flavorful.

Taro Nests

Large ('Betel-Nut') taro
Oil for deep-frying
Spoon-sized (2-inch-diameter) wire baskets on long (8–10-inch) handles

Shred taro in coarse, ideally long, strands. Spread on an open surface until strands are pliable and dry to the touch: one to several hours. Gather a heap into a large bowl; season*; toss to mix well. Twist and coil a wad of shreds lightly into a basket, lower gently into the hot oil, and fry until golden. Flip, withdraw basket leaving the nest to float, and cook. When uniformly browned, remove and drain.

Leave to air-dry until completely cool. Serve as snacks. These will keep indefinitely if stored in air-tight containers.

* Seasoning per 6 cups of shreds:
    1 tbsp soy sauce
    2 tsp rice wine or sherry
    1 tsp salt
    2 tbsp sesame seeds

Alternatively, the air-dried strands can be patted into and pressed between two wire colanders or strainers, and then deep-fried. This creates a crisp 'nest' that can be filled with a stir-fried or braised dish, of which seafood with a green vegetable, e.g. scallops and broccoli, is the most common.

ORIENTAL RADISH *Loh baak* 蘿萄

APPEARANCE: The hallmarks of this root are its large size (seldom less than 5 inches in length), smooth skin, and alabaster color. It is usually cylindrical, approximately 2 inches in diameter.

QUALITY: Heavy, unblemished individuals are best. Inside they should be solid, not fibrous, translucent white, and pungently fragrant.

COMMENTS: Botanically speaking, this and the small red salad radish are only different varieties of the same species. The Japanese call it *daikon*; some people, seeking a more familiar epithet, call it 'Chinese turnip' but a quick sniff and/or nibble will assure you that this is indeed a radish and not by any means a turnip. The flesh is crisp, juicy, mildly pungent in taste, and edible raw or cooked.

The Chinese perceive *loh baak* as a 'cooling', detoxifying vegetable with the ability to dissolve internal mucous. It is recommended for conditions of heat in the lungs (e.g. cough with mucous discharge) or of indigestion caused by eating too much rich, fatty food. By the same reasoning, it is cooked with fatty foods to provide balance and often for long periods, as in soup or braised dishes, to moderate its excessive cooling properties.

PREPARATION: Wash and scrape the surface lightly as a means of peeling; chop, grate, or shred as desired.

COOKING:

Western Westerners may enjoy this vegetable best sliced paper-thin in salads. It can also be pickled in vinegar with sugar and a little chilli. To pickle *loh baak*, follow the recipe for pickling stem ginger (p 112), but slice the radish in thin cross sections or shred it before salting.

For braising and boiling, use *loh baak* as you would potatoes. Combine it with carrots and beef to make a hearty winter soup, or braised, like stew, with cuts that require long cooking, such as shin of beef or pork skin. The radish withstands long cooking without disintegrating, absorbs the meat flavors, improves the sauce, and helps tenderize the meat.

Chinese *Loh Baak Go* is one of the most common concoctions made from this vegetable. A *go* is a stiff rice flour pudding that is mixed, steamed, cooled, then sliced in squares and fried just before serving. There are both sweet and savory types; *loh baak go* is savory, made of grated radish, and minced seasonings (see recipe following). Cantonese restaurants serve it as dim sum, while housewives prepare it to serve to guests and family at Chinese New Year.

Besides this, *loh baak* may be stir-fried, braised, or boiled. To stir-fry, first toss the prepared slices with (coarse) salt and let drain 10–20 minutes to keep it crisp; then cook with rich cuts of meat, seasoned with a highly flavored meat sauce or in the traditional combination of *loh-baak* with pickled pig's feet and fermented black beans.

HEARTY WINTER SOUP

1 Oriental radish, peeled and chopped in large chunks
Carrots, equal weight, similarly peeled and chopped
Soup meat or bones, beef or pork
(If using pork, you may add a small piece of fresh ginger, crushed; 3–4 Chinese dried figs, *mo fa gwoh* 無花菓 ; and a tablespoon of Chinese almonds/apricot kernels, *naam but hung* 南北杏)

Combine all ingredients in a large pot. Add 2–3 times as much water as volume of ingredients. Bring to the boil and simmer several hours until broth is well flavored and reduced to about 2/3 of its original volume. Season with salt and pepper.

BRAISED BEEF & RADISH

Oriental radish, peeled and chopped in chunks
Stewing beef, chopped in similarly sized chunks
5-spice powder (*ng heung fun* 五香粉), 1–2 tsp per pound of meat OR
    Star anise, fennel seeds, cloves, cinnamon, Chinese peppercorns

In a small amount of oil in a braising pot, brown meat. Add radish, powder or spices (in quantities to taste), and water to a depth of 1 inch. Cover and simmer gently until meat is tender. Adjust seasoning with salt or soy sauce, and serve.

RADISH PUDDING (*LOH BAAK GO* 蘿蔔糕)

5–6 lb radish
1 lb rice flour (*jeem mai fun* 粘米粉) (N.B. NOT glutinous rice flour)
4 sticks of Chinese sausage (*laap cheung* 臘腸) or about 1 cup Cantonese roast pork
    (*cha siu* 叉燒), fresh pork, or—as a last resort—ham
1/2 cup dried shrimp (*ha mai* 蝦米), soaked
5–10 winter mushrooms, soaked
1 strip Chinese preserved fat pork (*laap yoek* 臘肉) or 1 cup fat pork
2 dried halibut (*joh hau yu* 左口魚) or 1 stock cube
Garnishes: 1/4 cup preserved red ginger (*hoeng geung* 紅薑), finely shredded
          1/4 cup toasted sesame seeds

Soup stock: Toast halibut directly over a flame or under a grill, ignoring minor burns (to the fish, that is), and then simmer in around 4 cups of water for about 30 minutes.

Radish: Grate coarsely directly into a small amount of water; eventually the water should barely cover the volume of grated radish. Bring to the boil and simmer for about 15 minutes.

Other ingredients: Chop meats in small dice; chop mushrooms in even smaller dice, and mince shrimps.

Combining it all: Drain liquids from fish and radish into a large pot where they will cool. (Save the radish but discard the fish.) Put rice flour in a large bowl; add soaking liquid from mushrooms; then add the cooled, cooked stock gradually, stirring constantly. Top up with enough water to make a batter of medium viscosity. Season to taste with about a tablespoon of salt and some white pepper.

Combine batter, cooked radish, mushrooms, shrimp, sausage, and pork in large wok or pot. Heat, stirring constantly, until mixture begins to thicken. Pour into two oiled 10-inch-diameter x 2-inch-deep pans, or any number of smaller pans (such as cake pans) of the necessary volume; steam approximately 2 hours until thoroughly set.

The setup for steaming can be arranged in a number of ways. If your wok or pot is deep enough, set the bottom pan on a rack or brick and stack the other(s) above it by using two wooden chopsticks laid parallel across the rim of the bottom pan as a rack. Only the depth of your pot and supply of chopsticks limit stacking in this manner. If using a wok, you may lay a towel around the edge of the lid to reduce the escape of steam. In either case, check the water level periodically and add hot water as needed to maintain steady steam production.

Alternatively, you may bake the puddings in the oven. Use a low temperature such as 300°F, cover the pans with foil, and set a pan of water in the oven to create a moist environment.

When done, sprinkle the surface(s) of the puddings thickly with sesame seeds, scatter shreds of ginger over, and cook an additional 10 minutes.

The pudding may be served immediately but the more traditional procedure is to wait. When cool, cover with plastic wrap and store in the fridge—it will keep several weeks. To serve, slice it in 1/2-inch slabs, and pan-fry lightly, giving the outside a thin, crisp crust while softening the inside. Serve for breakfast, lunch, or snacks.

GREEN ORIENTAL RADISH *Cheng loh baak* 青蘿蔔

APPEARANCE: Like many of the white Oriental radishes, this vegetable is tubular, 6–8 inches in length, about 2 inches in diameter, and green, both inside and out.

QUALITY: Sound, heavy roots are best; examine the stem end in particular for signs of rot.

COMMENTS: This is another cultivated variety of the radish (alias *daikon* in Japanese). It has the same crisp texture and mild pungency of its siblings, but is a different color. And, like the other radishes, it is considered 'cooling' and detoxifying, but also potentially debilitating; hence it is always cooked well (2–3 hours) before serving and is invariably cooked with (nourishing) carrots—both procedures deemed to counterbalance its potentially harmful qualities.

COOKING:
Western This radish may be substituted for—or used in addition to—the small red salad radishes, although it is a bit more coarse both in texture and flavor.
Chinese The Cantonese invariably make this into soup. Beef, pork, or fish may be used; an equal volume of carrot is usually included—providing a balance of red and green, cooling and warming tendencies (if not also yin and yang); and such soups are most common during the winter months. The following is a tonic soup prepared by Cantonese mothers to help their families tolerate cold, dry weather:

MOISTURIZING SOUP
2 white-fleshed fish or fish tails (e.g. carp)
1/2 lb pork meat or 1 lb pork bones
1 green radish
Carrot (equal in volume to the radish)
3 dried Peking dates (*mut jo* 蜜棗)
About 2 tbsp Chinese almonds/apricot kernels (*naam but hung* 南北杏)

Scale, gut, wash, drain, pat dry, and rub the fish lightly with salt. Sauté vigorously in oil just until skin is golden. Peel radish and carrot and chop into large chunks. Combine all ingredients in a large pot with 2–3 times as much water. Bring to a boil and simmer until broth is milky white, well flavored, and reduced by about half. Season with salt and serve.

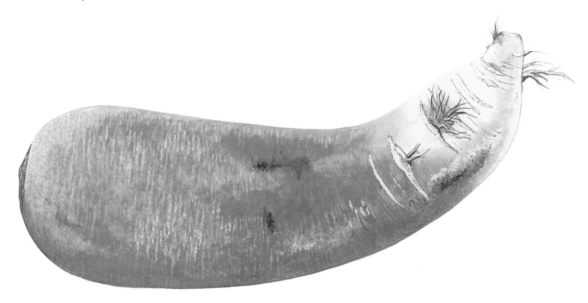

ARROWHEAD *Chee gwu* 慈菇

APPEARANCE: These vegetables resemble small eggs in size, shape, and color. They measure 1 inch in diameter and 2–3 inches in length, including the short shoot. The smooth, thin, beige skin distinguishes them from other root vegetables; the one or two fine, dark lines around their middles and lack of roots distinguish them from shallots and other onions.

QUALITY: Those with smaller shoots should be more tender and flavorful.

COMMENTS: As the North American name 'swamp potatoes' suggests, the arrowhead is a storage organ—technically known as a 'corm'—which grows under water. Like another veg of similar ilk, the water chestnut, its white flesh has a pleasant crunchy texture; the flavor starts off sweet, with a faint resemblance to fresh corn, but ends up bitter unless properly prepared.

According to chemical analysis, arrowheads are one of the most nutritious starchy vegetables in the market, being significantly higher in protein, minerals (particularly phosphorus), and fibre than either potatoes or taro. The Chinese reckon they are fairly balanced in terms of hot and cold, but warn those with constipation not to eat too many. In practice, arrowheads are served only occasionally, and primarily in the winter.

N.B. 'Arrowroot' is a different plant (*Calathea* sp.) from a different family (*Marantaceae*) grown in a different part of the world (the Caribbean), although its edible part is also egg-shaped and potato-like.

PREPARATION: Peel off the outer skin down to white flesh; remove the sprout. Either deep-fry quickly or boil, either whole or in slices, in order to remove bitterness. Then proceed with final cooking.

COOKING:

Western Use arrowhead as you would potatoes, but expect differences in taste and texture. They may be served whole like new potatoes; chopped and fried like hashbrowns; mashed; creamed; braised or baked. Overcoming bitterness is the cook's greatest challenge; seasoning with a pinch of sugar and/or herbs (particularly sweet, warm herbs such as oregano) and/or spring onions will help.

Chinese Arrowheads are typically prepared by braising: whole, with pork for richness, with soy sauce for flavor, and with a hefty pinch of sugar for balance. Vegetarians may do the same sort of thing, substituting gluten (*meen gun* 麵筋) for the pork.

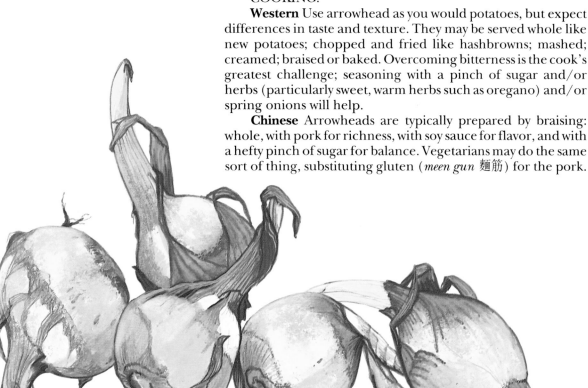

JICAMA   *Sa got*   沙葛

APPEARANCE: Among root vegetables, this is the only one with a narrow neck and lobed bottom. It varies from 3 to 8 inches in diameter, and its skin is sandy, both in color and texture.

QUALITY: Select sound, solid, worm-free individuals with the least convolutions (hence easier to peel). Larger ones give more edible matter for the peeling, and are no less tender than smaller ones.

COMMENTS: *Jicama* is its Spanish name, and tropical America is its homeland. Spanish explorers introduced it into the Philippines in the 17th century, whence it spread throughout Southeast Asia. The tubers are white, crunchy, sweet, slightly fibrous, and edible raw or cooked.

Jicama is basically starch: sweetness and fibre. It is low in vitamins but with a respectable amount of minerals and, interestingly, protein. The Chinese have virtually nothing to say about any more subtle properties. Hence, one is left to conclude that virtually any of the other flavors (salty, sour, bitter, pungent) can accompany it, and indeed must complement it for tasty results.

PREPARATION: Peel off the thick, sand-coloured outer skin together with the layer of white fibrous flesh just beneath it (if you grasp a corner and pull, much will come away in strips and pieces). Slice as desired.

COOKING:

Western Mexicans traditionally serve it drizzled with fresh lime and chilli-salt dip. Alternatively, serve it with any other dip as an appetizer, or tossed in salads. As a cooked vegetable, treat it like potatoes (e.g. cream, braise, boil, stir-fry). In either case, season it with pepper or lemon lest its sweetness seem out of place among the savories.

Chinese This is a homely vegetable that seldom sees the bright lights of restaurant kitchens. The most simple preparation is to stir-fry it in slices with beef, pork, poultry, or shrimp, either plain or with black beans and garlic. Jicama stir-fried in combination with squid and the sour preserved vegetable *haam suen choi* is a particularly compatible trio.

Alternatively—or when imagination fails you—substitute it for water chestnuts or bamboo shoots in more elaborate recipes. Jicama is certainly easier to prepare than either of those two, and finding its light, sweet crispness in a mixed dish can be a delightful encounter.

WATER CHESTNUTS *Ma tai* 馬蹄

APPEARANCE: About the size of ping-pong balls, these little devils can be unmistakably identified by skin color and the rings of papery leaf bases. When fresh from the swamp (where they grow) and lightly coated in dried mud, they may appear brownish-grey; when washed they are mahogany-black in color.

QUALITY: The best are large and round (hence easier to peel), firm and uniformly brown (hence sound).

COMMENTS: Water chestnuts are an ancient Chinese crop, believed to be some 3,000 years old. They are still common in markets in Hong Kong as well as in China, and still popular in homes, restaurants, and street stalls. Fresh *ma tai* have a crunchy, succulent texture and sweet nutty flavor that can be enjoyed raw or cooked.

Three characteristics may surprise the Western consumer. First, canned water chestnuts have but a shadow of the flavor of fresh. Second, cooked water chestnuts are more succulent than raw. When eaten raw, tasteless fibre remains in the mouth after the sweetness disperses; cooking renders the whole nut uniformly edible.

Finally, the Cantonese think of this first as a medicinal tonic, only secondarily as a vegetable. Chinese doctors describe water chestnuts as having 'cold' energy and sweet flavor—an unusually palatable cure for 'over-heated' conditions. Mothers reckon they are gentle enough for kids (who tend to overindulge in 'heating' fried snacks and candy bars), while children reckon they taste good enough to eat.

In cooking, the 'cold' energy of water chestnuts is modulated by long cooking or used for harmony in combination with warming foods, such as meats and onions.

The best method for storing these nuts is in a plastic box, which allows air to circulate among them. Although sound nuts will remain fresh almost a month in this way, it is wise to check your supply periodically in order to discard early rotters.

PREPARATION: Wash; peel (admittedly tedious, but necessary). The flesh should be pure white; if it is not (yellow is the typical color of decay), trim generously or discard completely because off-flavors from any rotten spots will travel quickly through the porous flesh. Soak immediately in water to discourage discoloration.

You may store peeled water chestnuts in a jar, covered with slightly salted or sugared water. Some flavor will leak into the water, but that is the price for the convenience of peeling them all at once.

COOKING:

Western Eat out of hand as a snack or dessert. Combine (preferably parboiled) in salads of fruit, greens, or other vegetables. Wrap in bacon, grill, and serve as an hors-d'oeuvre.

Chinese This is one of the very few vegetables that the Chinese (or, at least the Hong Kong Cantonese) eat fresh and raw. For snacking, street vendors sell skewers of 4–5 whole, peeled water chestnuts from large glass jars of sugared water.

Nevertheless, serving water chestnuts cooked is by far more common. They are used in sweet and savory dishes alike. On the sweet side, they are used in tonic dessert soups and puddings. On the savory side, they also figure in tonic soups (with esoteric parts of pigs), braised casseroles (particularly with lamb and leeks), stir-fried mixtures (particularly with broccoli and/or seafood), and minced concoctions for steaming (recipe below), pan-frying, or stuffing wonton (again, particularly with prawns).

Finally, water chestnut flour is the *crème-de-la-crème* for thickening sauces and shark's fin soup, because it develops a rich satiny sheen and smooth texture without interfering with the original flavor of the food it envelops.

MOOI CHOI JING YOEK BANG
Plum-blossom preserved cabbage (*mooi choi* 梅菜)
Water chestnuts, peeled, grated
Lean pork meat, minced
(Dried cuttlefish, soaked, cleaned, minced)
(Winter mushrooms, soaked, chopped finely)
(Chilli, fresh minced, powder, or sauce)

Use approximately equal parts of all ingredients with just a touch of chilli to taste. Rinse *mooi choi* well to remove excess salt; squeeze relatively dry and chop finely. Combine all ingredients and season with a dash of light soy sauce, a pinch of sugar, and a bit of cornstarch. Pat into a shallow dish or enamel pan; drizzle a little cooked oil on the top to seal in flavors and repel water vapor. Steam over boiling water or cooking rice until pork is done, 15–20 minutes.

Alternatively the mixture may be stir-fried or shaped into patties and browned like hamburgers.

POTATO & CHESTNUT PATTIES
Cooked potato (boiled or baked), mashed
Carrot, raw, grated
Water chestnuts, peeled, grated

Use approximately equal parts of all ingredients. Mix all together. Season with salt, pepper, and a dash of ginger juice or grated ginger; stir in a dusting of cornstarch (approximately 1 tsp per cup of mixture). Shape into small patties of 1-inch diameter. Pan-fry until golden on both sides.

BARLEY, BEAN SHEET, & WATER CHESTNUT SOUP
1/3 cup barley
1 fresh but dried soy milk sheet (*fu jook* 腐竹)
5–10 water chestnuts, peeled, quartered
1/4 teaspoon whole peppercorns (preferably white), crushed roughly

Put barley and peppercorns in approximately 3 cups of water; bring to the boil. As it froths, crumble in the bean sheet and then add the water chestnuts. Continue to simmer—with a gentle but decided bubbling action in order to dissolve the bean sheet—until barley has swollen, 1–2 hours. Season with salt.

SWEET POTATO *Faan su* 蕃薯

APPEARANCE: Literally hundreds of varieties of sweet potatoes are grown throughout the world, so tubers vary in size, shape, and color of flesh and skin as well as in taste and texture. Nevertheless, there are identifying consistencies. The skin is some shade of brown, and it is smooth, with hairlike roots. The shape is—most particularly, note—tubular and tapering to a point at both ends. Flesh color varies from white to deep orange to purple.

QUALITY: Tubers with purple flesh are considered the finest; those with deep orange flesh are generally more moist and sweeter than the pale varieties, which can be mealy and dry (but are considered to have more medicinal value). Check carefully for signs of rot, as these tubers do not keep well once out of the ground.

COMMENTS: Botanically, of course, sweet potatoes are not potatoes at all, nor are they yams, although all three can be cooked in much the same ways. Sweet potato is the oldest cultivated tuber of the trio, and it continues to be the most widely cultivated root crop in Southeast Asia.

Cooked sweet potatoes are starchy and soft, with a sweetness reminiscent of baked winter squash or roasted chestnuts. They can be dry or moist, smooth or somewhat fibrous in texture.

Although they use different terms, both East and West agree that the main nutritional value of sweet potatoes is in providing energy. The Chinese furthermore warn that eating too much can cause stagnation in the stomach. The antidote? Cook it by roasting; if boiling it, add ginger; or have it with a little wine.

PREPARATION: Scrub clean; leave intact for baking; or peel and chop for other purposes. If you peel them, soak immediately in water to discourage discoloration.

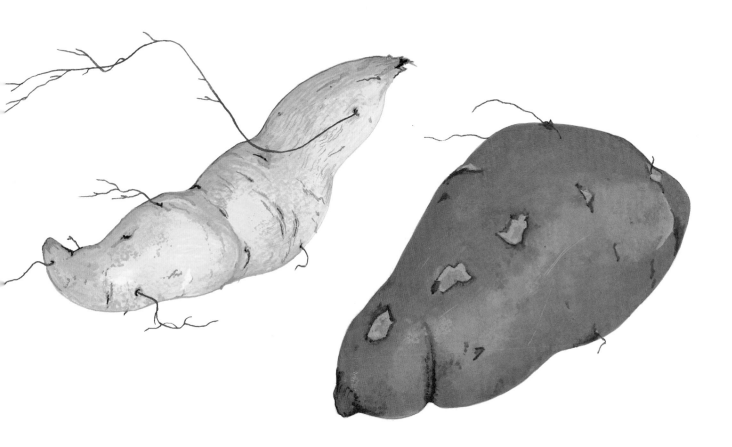

COOKING:

Western Like white potatoes, these may be sliced thinly and deep-fried; chopped and boiled; or baked or microwaved in their jackets. Once cooked, the flesh may be puréed, mashed, or sieved, seasoned and served as a savory vegetable or dessert (e.g. pie, tarts, tea breads). For the former, beat in salt, pepper, and sour cream or a dash of lemon juice. For the latter, sweeten with molasses or honey, add chopped nuts for texture, and cinnamon, nutmeg, and ginger for spice.

Chinese In Hong Kong, sweet potatoes are most often served sweet. Street vendors sell baked ones from portable ovens. Housewives make snacks and soups, as follows:

SWEET POTATO SOUP
Sweet potatoes
(Peanuts)*
Ginger

Chop potatoes coarsely (peeled or not, as you like). Use a small handful of peanuts per 3–4 cups worth of chopped potato; rinse them in hot water. Combine chopped sweet potatoes, peanuts, a thick slice of peeled, crushed ginger, and a pinch of salt in a large pot with 3–4 times as much water. Bring to the boil and simmer gently until tubers are quite soft and broth is well flavored.

* Peanuts (mainly the skins) are naturally slightly bitter. Hence adding them counterbalances the natural sweetness of the sweet potatoes and produces more of a savory soup, suitable for serving with a meal. The Cantonese, however, typically serve this as a dessert; hence they omit the peanuts and add slab sugar (*peen tong* 片糖) at the end.

DEEP-FRIED SWEET POTATO BALLS
Sweet potato
Sugar
Wheat flour or glutinous rice flour
Peanut butter
Sesame seeds

Boil sweet potatoes until soft (preferably with a crushed chunk of ginger). Mash flesh, season with sugar. Add enough flour to make a stiff dough. Pinch off a bit of dough; form into a flat circle, place a dab of peanut butter in the center, pull edges up, and seal into a small ball. Roll in sesame seeds; deep-fry until golden.

KUDZU   *Fun got* 粉葛

APPEARANCE: A combination of characteristics distinguishes this root from others. First, it is unusually large: commonly 10–15 inches but possibly greater than 2 feet in length. It is heavy. Its skin is coarse and scarred. Its shape is elongated, tapered at both ends, and irregularly convoluted in the middle. If it has been sliced, look for narrow, dark concentric rings—like tree rings—in the dry, white flesh.

QUALITY: Apply criteria as for other roots, selecting firm, sound individuals. Dirt and/or mold on any exposed surface is usually truly superficial, so can be cut off, leaving the rest of the root fit for consumption.

COMMENTS: The name *kudzu* is Japanese, although the plant itself is native to the Asian continent. It was cultivated as a staple food throughout Southeast Asia for centuries until more tender, tasty, and nutritious crops (like sweet potatoes) were introduced. Today, kudzu and related species are still being grown extensively throughout the world—but primarily as a cover crop to prevent erosion, improve the soil, and provide fodder for cattle, rather than to feed humans.

Like its cousin jicama, another root of the pea family, the flesh of kudzu is white and sweet; unlike the latter, it is not tender, moist, or edible raw. Hence the Chinese make soup with it while the Japanese process it into starch, which is used as a thickener. Why bother? one may ask. The answer lies in the subtleties of kudzu chemistry. It is reputed to have an exceptional ability to harmonize digestion, either soothing inflamed conditions or tonifying deficiencies—in other words, to cure whatever ails that particular part of one's anatomy.

PREPARATION: Slice, using determination and a sharp, thin knife. Peel. Chop coarsely.

COOKING: Fresh kudzu is strictly soup material, meaning the nourishment and flavor lies in what can be extracted by a long period of boiling, not in what can be chewed. Furthermore, the goodness is subtle in flavor; hence kudzu is usually a supporting ingredient rather than the main attraction in culinary productions.

The Cantonese recommend boiling kudzu with pork, or pork and fish, often with a combination of dried bits and pieces (e.g. tangerine peel, foxnuts, adzuki beans, Job's tears barley). Other cooks may simmer it with chicken or beef, or a combination of roots (e.g. carrot, potato, onion) for a vegetarian stock.

BONE-FIRE SOUP
Kudzu
Pork, meat or bones
Adzuki beans (*chek siu dau* 赤小豆)
Red dates (*hoeng jo* 紅棗)
Dried tangerine peel (*gwoh pei* 菓皮)

Combine everything in a large pot, using only a handful of adzuki beans and a few dates to substantial and equal proportions of pork bones and kudzu. Add water to cover all ingredients well. Bring to the boil, reduce heat, and simmer at least 2 hours until liquid is reduced by about half. Season with salt, and serve. Everything can be eaten, or not, as desired.

Appendix

The botanical names and historical information recorded here were gleaned primarily from *Vegetables in South-east Asia* by G.A.C. Herklots (1972), and *Tropical Crops: Monocotyledons* and *Tropical Crops: Dicotyledons* by J.W. Purseglove (1975).

PLANTS	VEGETABLES			
BOTANICAL NAMES	COMMON NAMES	CANTONESE PRONUNCIATION	CHINESE CHARACTERS	PAGE
FUNGI				
Agaricus campestris	Button or field mushrooms	Yeung kwun	洋菌	—
Auricularia spp.	Wood ear mushrooms	Wun yee	云耳	30
Lentinus edodes	Winter mushrooms	Doeng gwu	冬菇	28
Tremella fuciformis Berk.	Silver wood ear mushrooms	Ngun yee	銀耳	97
Volvaria esculenta	Straw mushrooms	Cho gwu	草菇	108
FLOWERING PLANTS				
MONOCOTS				
Alismaceae				
Sagittaria sinensis Sims	Arrowhead	Chee gwu	慈菇	121
Alliaceae (Onion Family)				
Allium ampeloprasum L. var. porrum (L.) Gay	Leek	Dai suen	大蒜	47
A. cepa L. var. *aggregatum* G. Don.	Shallots	Choeng tau	葱頭	22
A. cepa L. var. *cepa*	Onion	Yeung choeng	洋葱	—
A. chinense G. Don.	Kiangsi scallions	Kiu choi	蕎菜	46
A. fistulosum L.	Spring onions	Choeng	葱	21
A. sativum L.	Garlic	Suen tau	蒜頭	19
A. sativum L.	Garlic shallots	Suen jee	蒜子	23
A. sativum L.	Flowering garlic shoots	Suen sum	蒜心	45
A. tuberosum Rottl. ex Spreng.	Chinese chives	Gau choi	韭菜	43
A. tuberosum Rottl. ex Spreng.	Blanched Chinese chives	Gau wong	韭黃	44
A. tuberosum Rottl. ex Spreng.	Flowering Chinese chives	Gau choi fa	韭菜花	45
Araceae (Arum Family)				
Colocasia esculenta (D.) Schott	Taro	Wu tau	芋頭	114
Cyperaceae (Sedge Family)				
Eleocharis dulcis (Bur.) Trin. ex Hens.	Water chestnuts	Ma tai	馬蹄	123
Gramineae (Grass Family)				
Dendrocalamus spp.; *Phyllostachys* spp.	Bamboo shoots	Sun	筍	106
Oryza sativa L.	Rice	Mai	米	11
Triticum spp.	Wheat	Muk	麥	—
Zizania aquatica L.	Wild rice shoots	Gau sun	膠筍	105

PLANTS	VEGETABLES			
BOTANICAL NAMES	COMMON NAMES	CANTONESE PRONUNCIATION	CHINESE CHARACTERS	PAGE
Zingiberaceae				
Zingiber officinale Rosc.	Ginger	Geung	薑	17
Z. officinale Rosc.	Stem ginger	Jee geung	子薑	112
FLOWERING PLANTS **DICOTS**				
Amarantaceae				
Amaranthus gangeticus L.	Chinese spinach	Een choi	莧菜	50
Asclepiadaceae				
Telosma cordata (Burm. f.) Merr.	Night-fragrant flower	Yeh heung fa	夜香花	101
Basellaceae				
Basella alba L.	Ceylon spinach	Saan choi	潺菜	53
Brassicaceae (Mustard Family)				
Brassica alboglabra Bailey	Chinese kale	Gai laan	芥蘭	34
B. chinensis Jus. var. *chinensis*	Chinese white cabbage	Baak choi	白菜	29
B. chinensis Jus. var. *parachinensis* (Bailey) Tsen & Lee	Chinese flowering cabbage	Choi sum	菜心	27
B. chinensis Jus. var. *rosularis* Tsen & Lee	Chinese flat cabbage	Tai gu choi	太古菜	33
B. juncea (L.) Czern. & Coss. var. *rugosa* (Roxb.) Tsen & Lee	Mustard cabbages:			
	Bamboo mustard cabbage	Jook gai choi	竹芥菜	36
	Swatow mustard cabbage	Dai gai choi	大芥菜	36
	Sow cabbage	Jiu la choi	豬乸菜	—
B. oleracea L. var. *botrytis*	Broccoli	Gai laan fa	芥蘭花	—
B. oleracea L. var. *botrytis*	Cauliflower	Yeh choi fa	椰菜花	—
B. oleracea L. var. *capitata* L.	Head cabbage	Yeh choi	椰菜	38
B. oleracea L. var. *gongylodes* L.	Kohlrabi	Gai laan tau	芥蘭頭	41
B. pekinensis (Lour.) Rupr.	Peking cabbage	Wong nga baak	黃芽白	31
B. rapa L.	Turnip	Choi tau	菜頭	—
Nasturtium officinale R. Br.	Watercress	Sai yeung choi	西洋菜	40
Raphanus sativus L.	Radish (small red)	Hoeng loh baak jai	紅蘿蔔仔	—

PLANTS	VEGETABLES			
BOTANICAL NAMES	COMMON NAMES	CANTONESE PRONUNCIATION	CHINESE CHARACTERS	PAGE
R. sativus L. var. *longipinnatus* Bailey	Oriental radish	Loh baak	蘿蔔	117
R. sativus L. var. *longipinnatus* Bailey	Green oriental radish	Cheng loh baak	青蘿蔔	120
Caricaceae				
Carica papaya L.	Papaya	Mook gwa	木瓜	96
Compositae				
Artemisia lactiflora Wall.	White wormwood	Jun jiu choi	珍珠菜	58
Chrysanthemum coronarium L. var. *spatiosum* Bailey	Garland chrysanthemum	Tong ho	茼蒿	59
Lactuca sativa L. var. *asparagina* Bailey	Stem lettuce	Woh sun	萵笋	102
L. sativa L. var. *capitata* L.	Head lettuce	Sai saang choi	西生菜	—
L. sativa L. var. *crispa* L.	Leaf lettuce	Saang choi	生菜	55
Convolvulaceae (Morning Glory Family)				
Ipomoea aquatica Forsk.	Water spinach	Ong choi	甕菜	48
I. batatas (L.) Lam.	Sweet potato	Faan su	蕃薯	125
Cucurbitaceae (Melon Family)				
Benincasa hispida (Thunb.) Cogn.	Winter melon	Doeng gwa	冬瓜	75
B. hispida (Thunb.) Cogn.	Fuzzy melon	Cheet gwa	節瓜	77
Cucumis sativus L.	Cucumber	Cheng gwa	青瓜	—
C. sativus L.	Yellow cucumber	Wong gwa	黃瓜	81
Curcurbita moschata (Duch. ex Lam.) Duch. ex. Poir	Squash	Naam gwa	南瓜	88
Lagenaria siceraria (Mol.) Standl.	Bottle gourd	Wu lo gwa	葫蘆瓜	79
L. siceraria (Mol.) Standl.	Hairy gourd	Po gwa	蒲瓜	—
Luffa acutangula (L.) Roxb.	Angled luffa	See gwa	絲瓜	83
L. cylindrica (L.) M.J. Roem.	Sponge luffa	Soi gwa	水瓜	85
Momordica charantia L.	Bitter melon	Fu gwa	苦瓜	86
Sechium edule (Jacq.) Swartz	Chayote	Faat sau gwa	佛手瓜	82
Fagaceae (Oak Family)				
Castanea dentata	Chestnut (North American)	-		—
C. mollissima	Chestnut (Chinese)	Lut jee	栗子	98
C. sativa Mill.	Chestnut (European)	-		—

PLANTS	VEGETABLES			
BOTANICAL NAMES	COMMON NAMES	CANTONESE PRONUNCIATION	CHINESE CHARACTERS	PAGE
Leguminosae (Bean Family)				
Glycine max (L.) Merr.	Soy bean sprouts	Dai dau nga choi	大豆芽菜	67
G. max (L.) Merr.	Soy beans (fresh)	Mo dau	毛豆	64
Medicago sativa L.	Alfalfa shoots	Muk sook	苜蓿	54
Pacchyrhizus erosus (L.) Urban	Jicama	Sa got	沙葛	122
Phaseolus aureus Roxb.	Mung bean sprouts	Sai dau nga choi	細豆芽菜	65
P. aureus Roxb.	Mung bean vermicelli	Fun see	粉絲	30
P. vulgaris L.	French string beans	Yook dau	扁豆	—
Pisum sativum L.	Pea shoots	Dau miu	豆苗	54
P. sativum L. var. *macrocarpon* Ser.	Edible peapods	Hoh laan dau	荷蘭豆	63
Pueraria thunbergiana (Sieb. & Zucc.) Benth.	Kudzu	Fun got	粉葛	127
Vigna sesquipedalis (L.) Fruw.	Long beans	Dau gok	豆角	61
Nymphaceae				
Nelumbo nucifera Gaerth	Lotus root	Leen ngau	蓮藕	110
Onagraceae				
Trapa bicornis Osb.	Caltrops	Ling gok	菱角	100
Solanaceae				
Lycium chinense Mill.	Chinese box thorn	Gau gei choi	枸杞菜	52
Lycopersicon esculentum Mill.	Tomato	Faan kei	蕃茄	—
Solanum melongena L.	Eggplant	Ngai gwa	矮瓜	93
S. tuberosum L.	Potato	Su jai	薯仔	—
Capsicum annuum L. var. *grossum* Sendt.	Bell pepper	Cheng jiu	青椒	91
C. annuum L. var. *minimum* (Mill.) Heiser	Cayenne pepper	-		—
C. frutescens L.	Tabasco pepper	-		—
C. annuum L. (several varieties)	Chilli	Laat jiu	辣椒	26
Umbelliferae				
Apium graveolens L.	Celery	Kun choi	芹菜	103
Coriandrum sativum L.	Coriander	Yuen sai	芫茜	24
Daucus carota L. subsp. *sativus* (Hoffm.) Arc.	Carrot	Hoeng loh baak	紅蘿蔔	—
Petroselinum crispum (Mill.) Nym.	Parsley	Faan yuen sai	蕃芫茜	—

Glossary of Romanization of Chinese Names

B

Baak choi (Chinese white cabbage) 白菜

Baak dau gok ('White' long beans) 白豆角

Baat Bo Laat Jeung (Eight Treasure Hot Sauce) 八寶辣醬

Bing Tong (Rock sugar) 冰糖

Bun long wu tau (Betel-nut taro) 檳榔芋頭

C

Cha gwa (Pickled melon) 茶瓜

Cha siu (Roast pork) 叉燒

Chee bang (Dried persimmon) 柿餅

Chee geung (Stem ginger) 子薑

Chee gwu (Arrowhead) 慈菇

Cheet gwa (Fuzzy melon) 節瓜

Chek siu dau (Adzuki beans) 赤小豆

Cheng dau gok ('Green' long beans) 青豆角

Cheng gwa (Cucumber) 青瓜

Cheng jiu (Bell peppers) 青椒

Cho gwu (Straw mushrooms) 草菇

Choeng (Spring onions) 葱

Choeng tau (Shallots) 葱頭

Choi sum (Chinese flowering cabbage) 菜心

D

Dai choeng (Big spring onions) 大葱

Dai dau nga choi (Soy bean sprouts) 大豆芽菜

Dai gai choi (Swatow mustard cabbage) 大芥菜

Dai suen (Leek) 大蒜

Dau baan laat jeung (Broad bean chilli paste) 豆板辣醬

Dau fu (Bean curd) 豆腐

Dau fu gon (Dried bean curd) 豆腐乾

Dau fu pok (Deep-fried bean curd) 豆腐卜

Dau gok (Long beans) 豆角

Dau miu (Pea shoots/tendrils) 豆苗

Dau see (Fermented black beans) 豆豉

Doeng gwa (Winter melon) 冬瓜

Doeng Gwa Joeng (Winter Melon Pond) 冬瓜盅

Doeng gwu (Winter mushrooms) 冬菇

Doeng sun (Winter bamboo shoots) 冬筍

E

Een choi (Chinese spinach) 莧菜

F

Faan su (Sweet potato) 蕃薯

Faat choi (Seahair) 髮菜

Faat sau gwa (Chayote) 佛手瓜

Fun got (Kudzu) 苦瓜

Fun see (Mung bean vermicelli) 粉葛

Fu Gwa (Bitter Melon) 粉絲

Fu jook (Soy milk sheets) 腐竹

Fu yu (White fermented bean curd) 腐乳

G

Gai choi (Mustard cabbage) 芥菜

Gai laan (Chinese kale) 芥蘭

Gai laan tau (Kohlrabi) 芥蘭頭

Gau choi (Garlic chives) 韭菜

Gau choi fa (Flowering garlic chives) 韭菜花

Gau choi sum (Flowering garlic chives) 韮菜心

Gau wong (Blanched garlic chives) 韮黃

Gau gei choi (Chinese box thorn) 枸杞菜

Gau sun (Wild rice shoots) 膠筍

Geung (Ginger) 薑

Go (Rice pudding) 糕

Gong yiu chiu (Dried scallops) 江瑤柱

Gwoh pei (Dried tangerine peel) 蝦醬

H

Ha go (Fermented shrimp paste) 果皮

Ha jeung (Fermented shrimp sauce) 蝦糕

Ha mai (Dried shrimp) 蝦米

Haam daan (Salted duck egg) 鹹蛋

Haam suen choi (Salt-sour cabbage) 咸酸菜

Haap jeung gwa (Chayote) 合掌瓜

Hoeng geung (Candied red ginger) 紅薑

Hoeng jo (Red dates) 紅棗

Hoeng nga wu tau (Red-budded taro) 紅芽芋頭

Hoh fun (Wide rice noodles) 河粉

Hoh laan dau (Peapods) 荷蘭豆

Hon ong choi ('Dry' water spinach) 旱甕菜

J

Jai gai (Vegetarian chicken) 齋鷄

Jee geung (Stem ginger) 子薑

Jee jook (Soy milk sticks) 枝竹

Jee ma jeung (Sesame paste) 芝麻醬

Jeem mai fun (Rice flour) 粘米粉

Jeung yu (Dried octopus) 鱆魚

Joh hau yu (Dried halibut) 左口魚

Jook gai choi (Bamboo mustard cabbage) 竹芥菜

Jook sun (Summer bamboo shoots) 竹筍

Jun jiu choi (White wormwood) 珍珠菜

K

Kiu choi (Kiangsi scallions) 蕎菜

Kun choi (Celery) 芹菜

Kun lik (Perseverance) 勤力

L

Laap cheung (Chinese sausage) 臘腸

Laap yoek (Preserved fat pork) 臘肉

Laat jiu (Chillies) 辣椒

Lai fun (Rice vermicelli) 瀨粉

Leen jee (Lotus seeds) 蓮子

Leen ngau (Lotus root) 蓮藕

Ling gok (Caltrops) 菱角

Lo Hon Jai (Buddha's Delight) 羅漢齋

Loh baak (Oriental radish) 蘿蔔

Loh Baak Go (Radish Pudding) 蘿蔔糕

Lut jee (Chestnuts) 栗子

M

Ma poh dau fu 麻婆豆腐

Ma tai (Water chestnuts) 馬蹄

Meen gun (Gluten) 麵筋

Mo dau (Fresh soy beans) 毛豆

Mo fa gwoh (Figs) 無花果

Mo sun (Summer bamboo shoots) 毛筍

Mooi choi (Plum-blossom preserved cabbage) 梅菜

Mook gwa (Papaya) 木瓜

Mut dau (Honey peapods) 蜜豆

Mut jo (Peking dates) 蜜棗

N

Naam but hung (Chinese almonds/apricot kernels) 南北杏

Naam gwa (Squash) 南瓜

Naam jo (Black dates) 南棗

Naam yu (Fermented red bean curd cheese) 南乳

Ng heung fun (Five-spice powder) 五香粉

Nga choi (Mung bean sprouts) 芽菜

Ngaam chun daan (Quail eggs) 鵪鶉蛋

Ngaap sun (Duck gizzard) 鴨腎

Ngai gwa (Eggplant) 矮瓜

Ngun yee (Silver wood ear mushroom) 銀耳

O

Ong choi (Water spinach) 甕菜

P

Peen tong (Chinese slab sugar) 片糖

Pei daan (Preserved duck egg) 皮蛋

Po gwa (Smooth gourd) 蒲瓜

S

Sa got (Jicama) 沙葛

Saan choi (Slippery vegetable) 潺菜

Saang choi (Lettuce) 生菜

Saang gun (Deep-fried gluten puffs) 生筋

Sadeh jeung (Sadeh sauce) 沙爹醬

Sai yeung choi (Watercress) 西洋菜

See gwa (Angled luffa) 絲瓜

Siu ngaap (Barbecued duck) 燒鴨

Soi dau fu (Fresh bean curd) 水豆腐

Soi gwa (Sponge luffa) 水瓜

Soi ong choi ('Wet' water spinach) 水甕菜

Suen jee (Garlic shallots) 蒜子

Suen sum (Flowering garlic shoots) 蒜心

Suen tau (Garlic) 蒜頭

Suet lui hoeng (Preserved snow cabbage) 雪裏紅

Sun (Bamboo shoots) 筍

T

Tai gu cho (Chinese flat cabbage) 太古菜

Tong ho (Garland chrysanthemum) 茼蒿

W

Woh sun (Stem lettuce) 萵筍

Wong nga baak (Peking cabbage) 黃芽白

Wu haap (Taro nests) 芋蝦

Wu lo gwa (Smooth gourd) 葫蘆瓜

Wu tau (Taro) 芋頭

Wu tau go (Taro rice pudding) 芋頭糕

Wun yee (Wood's ear mushroom) 云耳

Y

Yau choi (Rapeseed) 油菜

Yeh choi (Head cabbage) 椰菜

Yeh heung fa (Night-fragrant flower) 夜香花

Yeung yee mai (Pearl barley) 洋薏米

Yook dau (String beans) 玉豆

Yuen sai (Coriander) 芫茜

Z

Za choi (Preserved mustard stem) 搾菜

Index